Contents

Dedication

This book honors the thirteen students I taught who died young but left a legacy of cherished remembrances for their families and friends. All thirteen taught me lessons about teaching and learning that continue to raise memories of them in my heart and mind. Their lives continue to be a blessing to all who knew them.

Ann Douglas Armel

Kent Barley

Susan Carter

Paul Cira

Nathaniel Davenport

Joan Devereaux

Matt Goff

Gordon Johnson

Reveley Lee

Susie Leinbach

Blair McWhorter

Elizabeth "Ibit'" Schutte

John Toxopeus

Introduction

This book is for teachers and their students. Its purpose is simple: to help teachers monitor and assess students each day. It's the assessments we complete in the short term that inform what and how we teach, because teaching is about unique children who bring diverse literacy skills to our classes. Daily and weekly assessments allow us to see this diversity as a strength and to use our knowledge of students' strengths and needs to make teaching and learning decisions.

This book, along with the rich array of assessment forms (more than 100 on the enclosed CD), will enable you to meet the essential elements of Response to Intervention (RTI). Along with the high quality reading and writing instruction you offer students, the forms in this book support tiered instruction and interventions. Completing the forms provides the documentation you need to match interventions to students' individual needs and continue monitoring students' progress. In addition, having the forms enables you to discuss students' progress with school administrators and with parents.

These daily and weekly assessments enable us and our students to observe progress that arrives in small increments but increases all year long as we work to build on each child's reading and writing strengths and needs. Yes, this book is for teachers and students. Its purpose moves us beyond monitoring students' progress to encouraging self-evaluation. Inviting students to reflect on and write about what they do well, and then, like learners young and old, confront and tackle their needs with the help of peers and teachers, can motivate students to become self-disciplined, productive learners.

Laura Robb

CHAPTER 1

Assessment Tools for Reading Comprehension

When I gave my sixth graders a choice between spending eight weeks on mystery stories or realistic fiction, the vote was unanimous: "We love realistic novels," echoed throughout the room as twenty students turned in their votes. This group of sixth graders attended Powhatan School, a rural independent school nestled between the Blue Ridge Mountains of Virginia.

I divided the unit of study into two parts: During the first five weeks, I grouped students according to their instructional levels and assigned each group one of the following three realistic novels: *Make Lemonade* by Virginia Euwer Wolff, *The Great Gilly Hopkins* by Katherine Paterson, and *Esperanza Rising* by Pam Muñoz Ryan. However, group instruction forces me to make accommodations regarding placement because I only have time to manage three groups. This means students reading a few months below the readability level of a book could be bumped up and given extra scaffolding.

During the last three weeks of this unit, each student read a realistic novel at his or her instructional level. This meant twenty different books, with each student learning at his or her instructional reading level. I collected books from the school library and my classroom—45 titles. Then, I sent students to different piles of books organized around reading levels. So, with the librarian's help, I made the initial selection, but students could choose from the stack of books that met their instructional needs. I call this type of instruction differentiated whole-class instruction. (See Chapter 4 of my book, *Differentiating Reading Instruction* [2008] for a full explanation of this process.) Now, however, I invite you to visit my class during the sixth week, when each student is reading a different realistic novel, and on a day when assessment takes center stage.

After reading aloud several pages from "Seventh Grade" from Gary Soto's *Baseball in April*, I focus the remaining 35 minutes of class time on assessment. Before class, on the chalkboard, I list the names of five students who will confer with me. Three will show me how they infer using a passage that's from their dialogue-rich books; two will discuss a major problem in their book and explain why it's realistic. I make conference decisions based on my observations of what students are practicing, because in addition to assessment, these meetings also offer me a chance to model and teach. While I confer, all but two students read their realistic novel.

In the back of the room, a pair of students shares an oversized pillow where they review and reflect on their journal entries, preparing to self-evaluate on the length and content of four weeks of journaling. The rest of the class finds comfortable reading spaces under their desks, against the walls, and on the remaining two pillows.

What I've described is some of the assessing that occurs in a differentiated reading classroom. There's always a mixture of me conferring, modeling, and providing support with students collaborating to discuss and reflect on their own work. In a differentiated reading classroom, using performance-based assessments—students' daily written and oral work—supports the instructional decisions that we make in order to improve students' reading, thinking, writing, and speaking.

Assessments for Differentiating Reading Instruction

Basically, we teachers have two kinds of assessments available:

◆ Performance-based assessments, also called formative assessments, are ongoing and review students' daily written and oral work, their behavior in learning situations, and teachers' observations of students. Quizzes, tests, and final exams become useful performance-based assessments only when teachers use them to determine students' strengths and needs, using results to plan scaffolds and interventions instead of simply giving a grade and moving on. The goal of performance-based assessments is to identify the support and instruction that will benefit students.

◆ Summative Assessments include norm-referenced tests, which give the rank of students as compared to the norm group. The Iowa Test of Basic Skills is an example of a norm-referenced test. Also included are criterion-referenced tests such as mandated state tests, which measure what students know about a particular subject, what skills they can perform, and how they compare to their grade-level peers. Criterion-referenced tests evaluate the effectiveness and strengths of a school's instructional programs. The goal of summative assessments is to judge students' achievement.

The state tests that all public school students must take offer teachers a glimpse of students' performance on one test completed in one to two days. For classroom teachers who make instructional decisions all day long, every school day, once-a-year measures cannot accurately inform daily teaching decisions. At best, by reviewing several state test results, we can track trends such as improvement or decline in comprehension, vocabulary, or writing scores. Trends provide general information about a child, but aren't helpful for those all-important daily decisions that grow out of the rich and varied work in a differentiated reading classroom, such as learning, practicing, and independently applying reading strategies to books they can read (Popham, 2003; Robb, 2008).

Performance-based assessments take into account the concepts and strategies we teach. Such assessments could be an informal journal response, a bookmark, discussions, book logs, oral book talks, written reviews, paragraphs and essays about reading, or projects such as Readers Theater presentations, puppet shows, and cartoons. When I say that studying process is the key to using assessments to make instructional decisions, it's because we teach process. True, the process eventually results in a product such as a final draft of an essay or the performance of a student-composed play. But it's during the journey toward the product that you and I teach and students practice and learn; it's the journey that lets us know what students did to create a product (Afflerbach, 2007). It's the process that informs our teaching and students' learning.

Let me give you a concrete example. Teachers in two different sections of eighth grade teach a unit of study on biography. The school requires all students to be able to create a thesis statement about the person, then support it in an essay using three to four pieces of evidence from their biographies. The thesis can relate to obstacles in the person's life or to events and relationships that helped this person reach a key goal.

One teacher assigns the task, gives a due date, and collects the final draft. Product-oriented, this teacher has no idea how students planned and developed this short essay. Students receive a letter grade and move on to another assignment. This might work for top students; it makes scaffolding or helping students who struggle with this task difficult because the process—how the student arrived at the final draft—is missing. In fact, the student might have composed the final draft the night before the assignment was due without thinking about process. Assignments that ignore process permit students to work without having their needs addressed. This can prevent progress.

The second teacher carefully thinks through the process for the same assignment because she understands that it's a knowledge and understanding of process that ultimately benefits her students. The teacher develops stages for students to complete—stages that she'll monitor so that by the time students are ready to draft, their thinking has been refined and revised. Here's the list of stages she compiles:

- create a thesis statement;
- jot down three to four pieces of detailed support from the biography;
- write a possible title that relates to the thesis;
- develop an introduction that ends with the thesis statement;
- complete a first draft that includes the introduction and the support; and
- work on a closing paragraph that leaves the reader thinking about the thesis.

With students, the teacher establishes a deadline date for each part of the process, so he or she can review students' work. Those who can move on do so; those who require scaffolding receive it before they draft their essay, ensuring that they have a better chance of succeeding at the task.

So, process is primary with performance-based assessment because observing process gives us the data to draw conclusions about whether students need more support, and helps to determine what kind of support would be helpful. The process you assess will emerge from your understanding of reading comprehension (see pages 11–12). The assessment forms in this book have grown from my beliefs about teaching reading, and I hope that they prove useful as you work to support the growth and progress of each student. (See Appendix C, pages 139–141, for a list of these forms on the CD.)

As You Continue to Read . . .

In this opening chapter, you will review some basic research on differentiating reading instruction, the concept of tiering, reading comprehension, and the need for ongoing assessment. I'll provide a summary of conference forms, checklists, and self-evaluations for required and tiered assignments and conferences. You'll also reflect on creating tests that assess what you teach and explore the strategies and skills that help students learn and understand. Finally, I'll include some management tips for finding the time for ongoing assessment, keeping track of the data, and interpreting assessments so you can plan instruction and scaffolding. The chapter closes with some professional study suggestions and a set of questions for discussion and reflection.

Grounding Assessment in Your Classroom

Now that you see the close relationship between assessment, your planning and teaching, and students' learning, it's clear that assessment is woven into every minute of class time. In this book, I isolate assessments to give you choices and to present different ways to study and evaluate what students do. The primary goals are to improve students' learning and achievement, deepen your knowledge of the wide range of assessments available to you, and help you gather data that informs your instruction. But keep in mind that assessment is integrated into the daily work of the classroom and is not an isolated event.

Research Supports Differentiating Reading Instruction

Carol Ann Tomlinson has led the way for teachers to differentiate instruction across the curriculum (Tomlinson, 1999; Tomlinson & Cunningham, 2003). I turn to her research again and again to clarify my understanding of what differentiation means in a reading and English language arts classroom. For Tomlinson, assessment plays a critical role in allowing teachers to differentiate the following:

- *content*, or the materials students use for learning information;
- *process*, or how students think through, plan, and manage time for an assignment, as well as how they self-monitor and self-evaluate their reading, writing, and thinking; and
- *tasks*, or the assignments students complete that result in a product such as a Readers Theater script or an essay.

By focusing on these three areas, we can decide whether our interventions and accommodations are helping students move forward. What follows is a quick review of the ideas presented by other researchers who have examined the need to differentiate reading instruction.

- The seven multiple intelligences that Howard Gardner identified (1999) point to the fact that students have varied learning preferences, and activities and tasks should tap into these different strengths: verbal–linguistic, spatial, logical mathematical, musical, interpersonal, body–kinesthetic, and interpersonal. It's beneficial to offer choice assessments that include the different intelligences such as Readers Theater, puppet plays, drawing, oral presentations, interviews, dramatic monologues, and panel presentations.

- The brain research conducted by David Sousa (2001) explains that for the brain to learn and remember information, teachers should help students connect facts to issues, stories, and patterns. Attaching facts about global warming to stories people tell, to the issue of why we need to slow down and stop global warming, and to the patterns we see with glaciers and oceans makes the facts come alive. By anchoring the facts in meaningful situations, students understand and remember them.

- Schema researchers noted that students arrive at school with different sets of stored experiences and knowledge, which affects their ability to read and construct meaning (Anderson, 1984; Clay, 1993; Duke & Pearson, 2002; Marzano, 2004; Robb, 2000, 2008). What students bring to a lesson, then, has everything to do with their level of comprehension and recall. That's why finding out what students know through preparation activities helps you decide whether to start a unit or delay it in order to enlarge students' background knowledge. For example, if a group of students has never read a biography, then it's crucial to build their experience with biography by reading two or three picture books and discussing the text structure and purposes of this genre.

◆ The research of Lev Vygotsky supports three aspects of differentiating instruction (1978).

1. *Meaningful Discussions.* Vygotsky believed that children learn best in social situations. Therefore, classes rich in meaningful discussions help students learn by doing what they love and are terrific at.

2. *Learning at Instructional Levels.* Provide instruction to students in their teaching zone, where they can learn and progress forward with the support of an adult or peer expert.

3. *Scaffolds and Gradual Release of Responsibility.* Through modeling, teachers support or scaffold students' learning, then gradually release the responsibility for the task to the student.

Your ability to differentiate reading instruction depends on having a rich array of ongoing performance-based assessments, such as students' written work, oral presentations, quizzes, tests, conferences, self-evaluations, and observational notes (McTighe & O'Conner, 2006; Tomlinson, 1999; Tomlinson & Cunningham, 2003). These assessments offer you the data needed to pinpoint what students do well and areas that require scaffolding. The forms you'll find in this book enable you to study, evaluate, and improve students' reading, writing, speaking, and thinking by focusing students' thinking and learning before, during, and after reading.

Defining Reading Comprehension

The definition of reading comprehension we work with impacts the kinds of assessments we develop and use. It's crucial that all reading assessments connect to a definition of reading (Afflerbach, 2007). My definition of reading comes from the research on reading and my forty-three years of experience as a reading teacher in grades four through eight. Here's how I define reading comprehension:

◆ Reading is an active process for the reader, who brings what he or she knows about a topic and genre to the text.

◆ Readers use specific skills and strategies to comprehend materials and to solve meaning problems they encounter.

◆ Reading involves decoding a text, but always with the goal of constructing meaning using what the reader knows.

◆ Developing a learner's vocabulary is an important aspect of reading because readers have to understand the meanings of words to comprehend texts.

◆ The purpose of reading is to understand and interpret the meaning of a text—this is comprehension.

- Thinking with text information asks students to make connections to a diversity of materials, including other books, television, film, and the Internet, and to issues, themes, and problems in order to develop new understandings.

- Learners read to meet both academic and personal goals. Therefore, attitudes toward reading, motivation, engagement, and success play key roles in determining the development of skilled readers.

Having a clear and detailed definition of reading enables us to truly assess what's taught and monitor how much students have learned and absorbed. That's why, at the start of the year, I encourage teachers to assess to discover students' feelings about reading, to gain insights into their interests, the skills and strategies they use, and to determine whether they have personal reading lives.

Tiering Students' Assignments

In the differentiated reading classroom, tiering starts with matching reading materials to students' instructional reading levels and helping them select independent reading materials that can be read with ease and therefore enjoyed. (Help students find "just right" books, which will be one or more years below their instructional reading level.) It's important to permit students to choose independent reading materials. Choice means that it's okay for a proficient reader to read a magazine, a graphic novel, or a book you might consider too easy. Students' personal reading choices mirror the way we choose reading materials. Reading levels vary because of interest, recommendations from others, and the desire to just pick an easy read.

The number of instructional and independent reading books students complete will differ depending on what they can do successfully; this is also an example of tiering. The daily assessments you review—assessments that support your instructional decisions for individual students—are an aspect of tiering because they enable you to adjust required and choice reading and writing tasks to ensure that students experience success and develop feelings of *I can do this well* (Guthrie and Wigfield, 2000; Guthrie, Wigfield, Metsala, & Cox, 1999; Robb, 2008a; Tomlinson, 1999; Wormeli, 2007).

Tiering required and choice tasks does not mean that some students do less, others more, or that some do simple, basic tasks while others have opportunities to think at high levels. Tiering choice tasks can ask all students to think at high levels, make connections, and analyze materials. For example, if one student chooses to design a cartoon while another writes an editorial, both are going beyond their texts and making connections to a theme and issue. Both should be asked to explain the big ideas in their work. The caution I offer is not to overload your proficient readers with extra or longer projects, but to add complexity to each required task by asking for high-level thinking (Armstrong, 2008; Sousa, 2001).

Tiering is an important aspect of differentiating reading instruction because you can individualize strategic reading practice. For example, after practicing inferring with fiction and nonfiction, you identify three students who require additional practice. While others read or move on to using context clues to figure out tough words, you can work five minutes each day with those three individually or as a group and reteach the inferring strategy. Reading and writing assignments can also be adjusted based on your assessments, ensuring that students are working at their instructional level so they can experience success and build their self-confidence. Success and self-confidence enable students to progress with reading and thinking about meaningful work, and to comprehend accessible and challenging reading materials (Robb, 2008; Wormeli, 2008).

Response to Intervention (RTI)

With the information and assessment forms in this book, you can monitor the daily and weekly progress of readers who struggle. You'll start by differentiating reading instruction and offering students books at their instructional reading levels, books they can read. You'll continue by tiering daily written work and tests, helping students experience success with varied learning tasks. Then you'll use observational notes and data collected on selected assessment forms in this book and on the CD to plan research-based interventions for readers who struggle and special education students.

It's important to have a written plan along with written documentation for students who you are monitoring using the Response to Intervention (RTI) model. The purpose of documentation is to catch students' lack of progress quickly, before it transforms into failure and lowered self-esteem. Here are suggestions that can support your efforts:

◆ Prepare a separate file folder for each student you are monitoring using the RTI model.

◆ Study students' written work and your observational and conference notes twice each month, then develop and continually adjust a bimonthly written plan (see Form 16 on the CD).

◆ Review your plan each week and adjust as needed. Adjustments can include changing the intervention, adding a new intervention, conferring with the student, conferring with colleagues who teach the student, and contacting parents so they can support your efforts by reading to their child and encouraging independent reading at home.

◆ Date each assessment and adjustment to your plan so you can reflect on progress.

◆ Check your data twice a month to ensure that each student is making progress. If, in a month's time, you observe little to no progress, meet with the child, your school resource person, and colleagues who teach the student to brainstorm other possible interventions.

Keep in mind what I repeatedly point out in this book: Student assessment occurs daily and is ongoing. Student assessment that's document with the forms I've provided can provide you with the insights needed to make informed decisions about how to help students enlarge their vocabulary, decode tough words, make connections, build their background knowledge, and improve comprehension.

Forms for Assessing Students in the Differentiated Reading Classroom

In the chapters that follow, I will discuss the benefits of a sampling of forms and make visible the process I use to draw conclusions about students' learning using this information. In addition, I have included on the enclosed CD additional assessment forms you can use. This large menu offers you choices that meet the needs of the population you teach. These include conference forms and checklists for the following:

- getting to know your students' attitudes toward and experiences with reading;
- monitoring students' knowledge of the reading and vocabulary strategies used before, during, and after reading;
- noting what you've learned about whether students have absorbed a strategy or skill by analyzing their writing about reading and about applying strategies;
- studying tests you've designed to assess students' application of a reading strategy;
- reflecting on the thinking students show you in their journal entries;
- scaffolding and reteaching;
- observing students during whole-class and small-group discussions, during silent reading, while they work in pairs or small groups on a project, and during tests and quizzes;
- assessing book talks and group projects such as writing and presenting plays, creating a newspaper, or writing a Web site blog;

A Definition of Conferring

In this book, conferences are short, focused meetings between the teacher and one student or a small group of students, between student partners, or among a small group of students. By short, I mean three to six minutes. Pinpointing a specific topic for discussion, such as finding big ideas or making connections to other texts, is key to keeping meetings brief. Conferences that cover several points and exceed the recommended time tend to derail because students cannot practice and process more than one to two needs. Moreover, long conferences often result in the rest of the class becoming restless and rowdy because their needs are not being met.

- assessing tiered learning tasks where you match the task to a student's ability to complete it successfully; and

- inviting students to complete self-evaluation forms.

In Appendix A, pages 135–137, you'll find a list of the strategies that have assessment forms in the book or on the CD. The list includes a brief explanation of each strategy.

In addition, there's a form that helps you interpret several assessments so you can plan individual and small group interventions.

By this time I'm sure that you're shouting, *There's no way I can find the time to do even half of these items!* Let me assure you that you can find the time. Also, if you are a novice with using and analyzing performance-based assessments, you should not consider doing all of this right away. The management suggestions that follow will offer ways for you to ease into using assessments—students' work and your conference and observational notes—to inform your teaching and to support students' learning.

Finding the Time to Document and Interpret Performance-Based Assessments

Whether you organize your instruction in a workshop setting or prefer another mode of organization, you can set aside time for assessing students. First, the work you ask students to complete—reading, writing, individual and collaborative projects, book talks, and reviews—are all assessments that you already read and evaluate. Now you can select some student work that you've already read to review and evaluate using the process discussed on pages 20–21. I recommend that you focus on work that reveals students' progress and their needs.

For example, let's take a look at three journal entries by an eighth grader named Justine. I find that I learn more by looking at a entries composed at different points in the year.

In Justine's August 29 journal entry (Figure 1.1), her class notes are accurate, and her reaction to the poem is honest. I expected her explanation of poetic justice to be more on target because in fifth grade she studied Greek mythology and the concept of the punishment fitting the crime. However, even after discussing the poem, I see that she needs additional help with the concept of poetic justice.

Justine completed her journal work for October 6 (Figure 1.2) after discussing narrative story elements with her group. Here she displays a solid understanding of antagonistic forces, and she can show the change in a character to support the idea that Amanda is a "round character." I noticed a confusion with "limited/omniscient point of view"; her explanation needs more detail. This is also a topic for our conference.

On October 13 (Figure 1.3), following a small-group discussion of antagonistic forces, round character, and point of view, Justine completed an entry for "On the Bridge." Justine shows a strong understanding of all the narrative elements discussed except "round character." Justine shows what Seth is like at the end, but she also needs to show his personality at the beginning and how it changed. Since Justine did this on her October 6 entry, I know that she can make the adjustment in a conference. I decide to divide the conference topics over two meetings because it's important to not overwhelm students with too many suggestions and risk them shutting down, making the conference unproductive.

Points to discuss in our first conference:

◆ Celebrate all of the positives noticed: support from story for antagonistic forces; choice of point of view (though no support for this choice).

◆ Work on showing a character is "round."

Points to discuss in our second conference:

◆ Work on understanding "poetic justice."

◆ If time permits, discuss limited/omniscient point of view.

After studying a sampling of Justine's journal entries for the first five weeks of school, I decided to hold a brief conference to help her with terms that we will use through this unit on the short story. As a result, she developed more confidence with sharing her ideas, which translated into active participation during small-group and whole-class discussions.

During sustained silent reading and when students work on writing, I find the time to hold three- to five-minute one-one-one and small-group conferences, or take observational notes. In a 45-minute class period, you can confer with four students and still have about twenty minutes left for mini-lessons, a read aloud, and vocabulary work. Doing this one to three times a week, depending on your comfort level, enables you to review and reflect on a variety of assessments. These meetings can occur regularly throughout the year, or you can set aside half of a marking period for conferring and observing, or do this every other week. The more you "kid-watch" (Goodman, 1985), the easier it will be to take observational notes, so you can narrow the focus of conference topics and keep conferences short.

Justine A   English   August 29

Poetic Justice

I think Poetic Justice is when a Poem is written about Justice.

"Bishop Hatto"
          by Robert Southey

narrative ballad
narrator
narate
narration

WOW, ok, that was kinda gross...
rats have beaty red eyes and
carry disease and are disgusting.

Poetic Justice - crime and punishment

Figure 1.1 Eighth grader Justine's first journal entry

"On the Bridge"

Justine A	October 13
Protagonist ·main problem	– Seth; Adam lied about him and caused him to get beat up
1 Antag. Force + how it worked against the protag.	– Seth because he was the one who wanted to be cool, ^image^ made him get beat up
Point of View	3rd person - limited
Round Character(s) and Why...	– threw away his shirt with blood on it – showed he didn't care
Climax	– when he walked away

"Amanda and the Wounded Birds"

Justine A	October 6
2 antagonistic forces and how each work against Amanda	– Amanda's mom was always doing traveling, guest shows, and lecturing - spending time (a lot) at Terri's house • suspect's Terri has a crush on her boyfriend - wouldn't be friends? (she wonders) - how could Terri and Amanda not be friends? (she wonders)
Prove she's a round character by showing a change start-end	– became more confident that she could talk to her boyfriend
Point of View - limited - why - omniscient - why	- limited, she's telling the story

Figure 1.3

Another journal entry from Justine exploring antagonistic forces, point of view, and round characters

Find a rhythm and routine that works best for you and your students. However, before you arrange your schedule, make sure you read the following suggestions for getting started—suggestions that provide reasonable guidelines for building a wide range of performance-based assessments that can inform your instructional decisions.

Student-Teacher Conferences: A Key Assessment Tool

For me, a one-on-one conference is an important assessment tool because it provides insights into how students apply a reading strategy, how they use context clues to figure out tough words, what they write about their reading in journals and essays, and their performance on tests and quizzes. In addition to informing instruction, the assessments you collect and interpret become documentation for conferences with parents or administrators. For example, if a student has difficulty with inferring or synthesizing, your assessments provide the data needed to respond to this need with extra conferences, several sessions with your school's reading specialist, or some after-school assistance.

You can hold a conference with a student on any assessment. During a conference, you can probe into students' thinking and process to discover ways you can scaffold their learning and move them to independence. Conferences give you the chance to praise and celebrate excellence, but also help you understand the student's process. As you explore the book and CD, you'll discover six types of conferences (see below) that enable you to clarify an assessment, gain insight into students' instructional and independent reading, and/or use conference data to evaluate students' strengths and needs.

- *Getting-to-Know-You Conference:* Discuss information gathered through a variety of surveys and students' writing about their reading.

- *Reading Strategy Conference:* Observe how students apply a specific strategy to figure out what they do and don't understand about it.

- *Book Conferences: Fiction and Nonfiction*: Discuss students' independent reading.

- *Discuss-an-Assessment Conference:* Focus on a piece of writing, your observations of a student discussing a text, a test, or a quiz to better understand a student's process.

- *Scaffolding Conference:* Work with individuals or small groups to support them with any reading or writing task.

- *Reteaching Conference:* Help an individual or a small group of students understand a strategy, concept, or writing task by finding a different way to explain the process.

Getting Started: A Suggested Time Line

I urge you to avoid giving into teacher feelings of *I have to do it all*, especially if you're new to the profession. Keep in mind that the written work students do is part of performance-based assessment, so you're on your way. Here are suggestions for pacing yourself and keeping those anxiety and stress levels low.

First-Year Teachers: In addition to studying students' oral and written work, I recommend that you integrate three kinds of assessments into your repertoire:

The assessments you choose to collect and study will vary and change during each marking period because your assessments grow out of your teaching and allow you to gain insights into what and how students are learning.

- assessments such as interest and reading surveys, which provide insight into students' interests, their personal at-home reading lives, and whether they have a toolkit of strategies for solving reading problems;

- conferences to monitor how students apply one reading strategy in each part of the before, during, and after framework; and

- student self-evaluation of one key reading strategy.

Teachers With Up to Five Years' Experience: You'll do everything suggested for first-year teachers plus these assessments:

- conferences that monitor all the strategies that you are teaching and students are practicing;

- tests that reflect what you are teaching;

- observational notes, starting with one student and adding more as you feel comfortable; and

- student self-evaluations of the reading strategies you teach and their journal entries.·

Experienced Teachers: Complete as many of the assessments listed on page 14 as you need in order to understand how to support your students' needs.

These suggestions are exactly that—suggestions. Don't feel bound by them. You might feel comfortable doing more or less. Remember, you are the decision maker and know best how much you can juggle with all your other responsibilities.

Keeping Track of Students' Assessments

For me, the best way to keep track of assessments for each student is to store them in dated order in a file folder. If you teach a self-contained class, it's easy to store assessment folders in a file cabinet or a plastic crate. Middle school teachers who see three to five different classes daily can file two sections in one plastic crate. File all observational notes,

How Often Do I Evaluate Assessments?

If you teach middle school and have more than one hundred students, it's daunting to think of ongoing assessment for each one. Start with students who are reading two or more years below grade level or students with diagnosed learning disabilities and review their assessments every two to three weeks. Try to review the assessments of other students at least once during each marking period. Stagger reviews so that you read several a week. Begin this review after the third week of each marking period, for it's important to honor the progress of those who experience success. Moreover, you might discover an area where one of your best students needs some support. For example, sixth-grader Tanisha was able to find themes of short stories her group read but struggled with identifying the big ideas in informational articles about the rain forest. I noticed this while conferring with Tanisha and asking her to show me how she discovered big ideas. Over the years, I've learned *not* to assume that if a student can think in one area, the thinking process would automatically transfer to another. Scaffolding and working with a peer expert helped Tanisha think deeply about informational texts.

As you read on, you'll explore guidelines for thoughtfully studying and evaluating students' assessments—guidelines that invite you to slow down, be reflective, and draw conclusions about the assessments you're reviewing. This process differs from the split-second decisions we must make during each teaching day, such as giving a student more time to complete an assignment or finish a test or work with a different partner. Though split-second decisions are a reality of the teaching life, the reflective process that follows allows you to use what you know about reading and thinking to consider a range of possible interventions.

conference forms, and self-evaluation forms in the folder (see page 42). Select key pieces of written work and journal entries—pieces that show needs and progress.

Each time you set aside time to review and analyze a series of assessments, place a dated sticky note on the back of the last paper in the group. Having the sticky note quickly lets you know which assessments you've reviewed without having to remember the last paper read in every folder. This allows you to choose whether to look back at past assessments in addition to studying current ones or to focus on data only from the latest assessments.

Completing and collecting assessments is a first and important step because it's helpful to have a variety of student work to draw from as you make decisions about scaffolding, reteaching, and adjusting instruction and students' requirements. In the next section, I've outlined a process for evaluating assessments and included a form you can use to document your inferences and instructional interventions.

Guidelines That Work for Interpreting Assessments

What to do with assessments once we've collected them can feel overwhelming unless there is a process in place that can guide your thinking and evaluating. Without such a process, teachers I know simply store their performance-based assessments in a folder and never review them. I've developed guidelines that work for me. You might have to tweak or even eliminate some steps; that's okay as long as you use collected assessments to inform instruction and decisions to scaffold.

Guidelines for Evaluating Students' Assessments

1. *Review students' work.* Reread what you collected to refresh your mind.

2. *Take notes.* Do this for guidelines 3 through 6. As you study the assessments, use the form on page 27 (Form 15 on the CD) to jot down your thoughts. Documenting these assessment reviews enables you to refer to them later in the year and gives you data to share with administrators, parents, and the student.

3. *Draw conclusions about what the student does well.* Start with what the student does well and understands. Knowing this can help you figure out the kind of support that would benefit the student because you can make connections to areas of strength.

4. *Draw conclusions about areas that need support.* Use the questions on page 22 to help you make inferences, especially if the areas of need aren't apparent to you.

5. *Develop a plan of possible action.* In your notes, include more than one

intervention, instructional adjustment, and idea for scaffolding. This way you have ideas to fall back on if what you try first isn't helping the student improve. Always start with some positive comments, then move to the intervention.

6. *Review assessments with the student.* Ask, "How do you think I can help you with _____?"

By the middle grades and definitely in middle school, students have an idea of what kind of help they need or what they can and can't do well. For example, when I asked sixth grader Robert how I could help him improve his reading, he answered: "I need more words and need to read faster. It takes me forever to finish reading homework." Robert was on target. Since he was reading two years below grade level, Robert constantly worked at his frustration level with school assignments. He recognized that he could not pronounce many new words, nor understand their meanings. Weak word knowledge combined with more complex syntax in grade-level texts convinced Robert that no matter how hard he tried, he couldn't do the work.

Of course there will be times when students have no clue as to why some areas of learning are tough for them. That's fine. However, always set aside time to review the assessments with students to see what they have to say about their needs and successes. Self-evaluations will also provide glimpses into students' strengths and areas of need.

To Confer or Not to Confer

You won't have time to confer with every student after reviewing assessments. I try to confer once during a semester or trimester with every student. Meetings with students who are successful are brief; however, they need to receive feedback from you to boost their self-confidence and stretch their thinking.

Students who "get it" can self-evaluate (see Forms 76–98 on the CD) or discuss their work with a peer. Many times you'll find that making the rounds, pausing a few minutes at each student's desk to point out what's working and what needs additional attention, will suffice. Other times, you'll ask students who understand how to apply a reading strategy or figure out unfamiliar words using context clues to confer with a partner. It's helpful to have partners document their discussion on a piece of notebook paper and turn it in to you.

What to Do When Students Don't Get It

It's easy to feel frustrated when reteaching doesn't improve a student's learning. Most often, this frustration occurs when teachers reteach using the same lesson that the student didn't understand initially or after a second try. Reteaching is challenging because it asks us to move out of our comfort zone—the lesson we developed—and create another way to present a concept or strategy. However, changing the approach of a lesson is crucial for successful reteaching. My advice is to think about how the student learns best. Use these queries to help you figure that out, then adjust your lesson:

◆ Does the student learn better if I sit side-by-side him or her?

◆ Does the student do better reading the material twice?

◆ Is it helpful to have the student think aloud so I can understand the process being used?

◆ Should I have the student observe my process again and ask questions?

◆ Does the student need to write or draw in order to understand?

◆ Can the student tell me what was confusing about the lesson?

◆ Do I need to use an easier text?

◆ Would it be helpful for the student to work with a peer expert?

> ## Scaffolding and Reteaching Suggestions
>
> To give you extra support with reteaching, in the chapters that follow you'll find charts that describe students' behaviors that you may notice while discussing assessments or while observing students at work. I've included suggestions for scaffolding and teaching that you'll be able to use and adapt as you support students.

Creating Tests in the Differentiated Reading Classroom

Though tests are a more traditional form of assessment, they also work when you organize your teaching around differentiated whole-class instruction. With each student reading a book at his or her instructional level, you can still test students' knowledge of text structure, and their ability to apply reading strategies and answer open-ended interpretive questions (see Forms 67–72 on the CD). You'll do this by asking students to use their instructional and/or independent reading books to respond to questions or prompts such as:

◆ Name the protagonist, describe one key problem faced, and discuss the outcome.

◆ Choose an action or decision the person in your biography made, and draw conclusions about that person's personality.

Whatever you're teaching can be tested this way: relating an issue to a book, finding themes or main ideas, figuring out what information is important, or making personal, community, or world connections to the reading. Testing what you teach will be one of the assessments that you collect—assessments that enable you to evaluate students' needs and adjust assignments and instruction.

Evaluating Students' Assessments in Action: Grade 6

Now, let me walk you through an assessment review of a sixth grader that I completed after four weeks of school, so you can step into my process and thinking. The review focuses on Annie's ability to make inferences about characters' personalities, decisions, and interactions with others. I made the decision to do this review early in the year because Annie was reading three years below grade level and my observational notes confirmed this need. In addition, I focused my attention on her because I knew that she and three other students would need additional support with making inferences because of their reading levels.

Figure 1.4 contains my observational notes, which I've rewritten neatly using whole words instead of abbreviations. I decided to study Annie's assessments because I noticed during paired discussions of my real-aloud that she was unable to infer with text. On September 17, Annie could tell me that the author doesn't state the inference, but that Annie has to "think it." This let me know that Annie was starting to absorb the "what-it-is" of the strategy, but she needed to learn the "how-to-do-it" of the strategy.

These notes document the movement from not being able to infer to inferring with illustrations. It was this change along with observations during read-aloud discussions and pair-shares that helped me conclude that I needed to confer with Annie. Figure 1.5 documents the strategic reading conference in which I asked Annie to tell me what she knows and understands about making an inference. Then, I invited Annie to infer using a page from her instructional reading book. Note that Annie cannot use words to describe inferring and she can't infer the feelings of the four cat children who fly away and leave their mother behind.

Next, I wanted to pinpoint ways to support Annie early on, since she would need to infer in all our units of study (see Figure 1.6). I reviewed and studied Annie's journal entries, my observational notes, and the strategic reading conference, and developed three possible ways to support her. I try to offer more than two kinds of interventions just in case some don't work. It's also important to ask students "How can I help you?" Note that Annie provided me with a terrific strategy, and I started practicing inferring with her for a few minutes three times a week.

9/10   Annie

Situation: Discussion during Read Aloud
- raises hand all the time
- could not explain what an inference is
- discussed physical traits when asked to explain + give an example of personality traits

9/17   Annie

Situation: Discussion during Read Aloud.
- retells instead of using details to infer
- Knows making inferences means that "the book doesn't tell it - you have to think it."

9/20   Annie

Situation: Pair-Share to Get-Ready-to-Read Cat wings. (Ursula Le Guin)
- about cats with wings (cover)
- could not explain "fly-by-night."
- Prediction: about a mother cat + her 4 cats that have wings.

9/27   Annie

Situation: Pair-Share Catwings by Ursula Le Guin
- Inferred w/illustration on page 14. "Harriet's scared." When I asked for proof - " Dog chasing her."

Figure 1.4 *My observational notes on a sixth grader's ability to infer*

9/27   Annie

Journal Work:
- Retells w/many details.
- Infers from some Pictures in Catwings.
- Doesn't infer from dialogue or events.

Student's Name _Annie_____ Date _9/25____

Strategic Reading Conference

Directions: Jot down notes based on the conversation between you and your student,
using the questions below.

Title and Author _Catwings by Ursula LeGuin_____

Reading Strategy: Making Inferences

How can this strategy help you understand what you read?

Not sure. (Shrugged Shoulders)

What other strategies do you use while you read?

I predict — sometimes

How do you apply this strategy when you read?

I do it before (she reads)
when teacher tells us

Find a page in your book and think aloud to show me how you apply the strategy.

Catwings by Ursula Le Guin
Page 16- # where 4 cat-children fly away +
    have to leave their mom behind
Annie: They're starting a new life.
Robb: How do they feel? - (long pause)
Annie: Don't know

*Figure 1.5 Notes from my strategic reading conference with Annie, which I focused on inferring;
this form appears as Form 17 on the CD*

Student's Name _Annie_____ Date _9/30_____

Evaluating Student Assessments

Check the assessments you plan to review. Note any not on this list.

_____written work   ✔ conferences   _____tests

✔ journal entries   _____self-evaluations   ✔ observations

_____interest survey   _____reading survey   _____checklists

_____questions about reading

Directions: Jot down notes on this form as you review and study the assessments.

Draw conclusions about what the student is doing well.
- can explain that you "can't find inference in book-'cause author doesn't write it. I got to find it."
- Can infer from illustration
- is a good listener during read alouds

Draw conclusions about areas that need support.
- Annie needs to learn to infer from events and actions and from dialogue.

Develop a plan of possible action including interventions, instructional adjustments, and scaffolding.

1. Meet 3 times a week for 5 min. at a time & think aloud to show Annie how I infer.

2. Gradually release process to her.

3. Use real life situations & help Annie infer from these.
   inferring

Review work with the student and ask, "How can I help you with____?"
Annie: Do it with me.

Figure 1.6 My assessment review of Annie, completed after evaluating her journal work, observing her, and having a conference; the form appears as Form 15 on the CD and as a reproducible on page 27

Student's Name _____ Date _____

Evaluating Student Assessments

Directions: Check the assessments you plan to review. Note any not on this list on the blank space below. As you review them, record your observations and conclusions below.

_____ written work   _____ conferences   _____ tests

_____ journal entries   _____ self-evaluations   _____ observations

_____ interest survey   _____ reading survey   _____ checklists

_____ questions about reading _____ practice sheets   _____ _____

Directions: Jot down notes on this form as you review and study the assessments.

What is the student doing well? How do you know?

In what areas does the student need support? What assessment(s) indicates this?

Develop a plan of possible action including interventions, instructional adjustments, and scaffolding.

In a conference, review work with the student and ask, "How can I help you with _____?"

If the student doesn't need to confer with you, note whether he or she will self-evaluate or discuss with a peer and complete a peer evaluation form.

A key aspect of gathering assessments are the daily observations I make, which help me identify students' needs before I read a journal entry, test, or essay. In addition, becoming lifelong learners by attending conferences and reading professional books and materials enlarges our background knowledge, helping us interpret students' assessments and make daily decisions about scaffolding needs.

Professional Development Suggestions

In order to develop a solid foundation for using performance-based assessments, it's important to broaden and deepen your theoretical knowledge by reading professional journal articles and by organizing a study group to read and discuss a book the group chooses. The more background knowledge you have, the better you'll be able to make those instant and reflective decisions because you'll be drawing from a large and diverse knowledge base.

Professional Books

- *Checking for Understanding: Formative Assessment Techniques for Your Classroom,* ASCD, 2007.
- *Conferring With Readers: Supporting Each Student's Growth & Independence* by Jennifer Serravallo and Gravity Goldberg, Heinemann, 2007.
- *Fair Isn't Always Equal: Assessing & Grading in the Differentiated Classroom* by Rick Wormeli, Stenhouse and NMSA, 2007.
- *No Quick Fix* edited by Richard I. Allington and Sean A. Walmsley, Teacher's College Press, 2007.
- *Understanding and Using Reading Assessment, K–12* by Peter Afflerbach, IRA, 2007.

Professional Articles

- Articles on Informative Assessment in *Educational Leadership,* Vol. 65, No. 4.
- Articles on Assessment to Promote Learning in *Educational Leadership,* Vol. 63, No. 3.

In addition, I recommend that at team, department, or faculty meetings, teachers take turns bringing in students' written work and teachers' observational notes to discuss. Doing this develops your expertise with identifying students' strengths and needs by studying various artifacts.

Your librarian, reading resource teacher, literacy coach, lead teacher, or classroom teacher can and should suggest professional materials for study. The box on page 28 provides a starter list of professional books and articles.

Continue to Reflect and Wonder . . .

Before you move on to the chapters that contain forms along with student examples and analysis, I invite you to think about the questions that follow by discussing them with a colleague or mulling them over on your own. Return to these periodically to check on your progress using performance-based assessments.

- ◆ Why is it important to collect assessments frequently?
- ◆ What kinds of performance-based assessments are you collecting?
- ◆ How do you organize the assessments you collect?
- ◆ Why is it important to reflect on a diverse range of assessments in order to draw conclusions about a student's performance?

CHAPTER 2

Assessments That Help You Know Your Students as Readers

During my early years of teaching, my colleagues and I were all told to start covering curriculum by the second day of classes. Start covering curriculum, give homework, don't waste a day of instructional time—that was the administration's mantra. At that time I was teaching fifth grade, and I recall thinking, *I hardly know my students' names, and yet we're asked to plunge into rigorous work.* Each year, my level of dissatisfaction rose with this method of opening the school year. Finally, I created my own system and worked diligently, modeling routines I wanted students to understand and taking a variety of assessments, such as interest and reading surveys, questions about their reading lives, and conferences. My goal? To get to know my students as readers, writers, family members, friends—as the unique human being each one was. The more you're tuned into each student's strengths and needs, the better equipped you will be to support them.

Let me explain why getting to know each one of your students is important. When you need to discover your students' different instructional reading levels, it's essential to find out more about their personal and school reading lives, for this information can assist you as you estimate reading levels at the start of the year. Once you know the title and author of a book, you can check its Lexile level, which can help you estimate instructional reading levels (see box below). For example, if one sixth grader told you that in fifth grade her last instructional book was *Midnight Fox* by Betsy Byars (Lexile 970) and she loved reading *M.C. Higgins, the Great* by Virginia Hamilton (Lexile 620) on her own, that information along with standardized testing, surveys, and a getting-to-know-you conference could support your estimation of her instructional reading level.

Knowing your students' interests will help you suggest reading materials to them as well as choose pieces to read aloud. Setting aside two to three weeks to get to know your students also allows them to get to know you as a reader, a teacher, and a person as you

Lexiles Help You Match Readers to Texts

Lexiling books is one way to determine readability levels and helps you, with a great deal of accuracy, take the guesswork out of matching readers to books.

You can use the free Lexile Book Database at www.Lexile.com to offer your students choices within their instructional reading range. The chart that follows gives you grade levels, Lexile levels, and Scholastic Guided Reading levels. The overlap in Lexile levels provides you with more exact readability placements in a specific grade. For example, in fifth grade, the lexile range of 700 to 1000 lets you know the range from beginning grade-level readers (700 range) to proficient, above-grade-level readers (1000). When choosing books, it's important to consider readability as well as the topic and concepts. For example, *The Giver* by Lois Lowry (Lexile 760) has a readability level of fifth grade. However, the concepts and content are inappropriate for fifth graders, but appropriate for eighth grade and up.

For proficient readers in seventh and eighth grade, consider the topic, concepts, syntax, and vocabulary of a text. The following chart will support your estimate of instructional reading levels and text choices for students in grades seven and eight who are reading below grade level.

Grade Levels	Lexiles	Guided Reading Levels
First Grade	200–400	A to E
Second Grade	300–600	F to J
Third Grade	500–800	J to Q
Fourth Grade	600–900	M to T
Fifth Grade	700–1000	Q to V
Sixth Grade	800–1050	T to Z

will model how you answer questions or complete parts of surveys. During this time, you can establish routines and negotiate behavior guidelines that are part of differentiated reading instruction (see my *Differentiating Reading Instruction* [2008a]). Moreover, during these opening weeks, in addition to collecting assessments and conducting conferences, you can lay the foundation of your first unit by using your instructional read-aloud to introduce the genre, issues, and text structure you will be working with.

As You Continue to Read . . .

This chapter includes a discussion of assessments you'll explore in this book and on the CD. You'll read about assessments that can help you estimate each student's instructional reading level so that you can meet students where they are and carefully

move them forward. This is the heart and soul of whole-class differentiated reading instruction (see Chapter 4 of my book, *Differentiating Reading Instruction* [2008a]). You'll also learn how to interpret the assessments that you collect, then store them in a literacy assessment folder. I've included a quick and easy way to complete an oral error analysis and retelling so you can take a closer look at students whose instructional reading levels you're unsure of. Next, you'll learn the benefits and how-to's of taking observational notes as students read, discuss, and listen to your explicit lessons

---

Another Way to Find Instructional Levels

If you need to double-check whether the instructional match is a good fit or if you are unsure of a student's instructional reading level, use the oral reading error analysis described on pages 38–42.

Forms for Chapter 2 That You'll Find on the CD

Getting-to-Know-You Forms

- Reading Survey (Form 1)
- Eleven Questions About Reading (Form 2)
- Interest Inventory for Grades 4 and 5 (Form 3)
- Interest Inventory for Grades 6 and up (Form 4)
- What's Easy / What's Hard: Reading (Form 5)
- What's Easy / What's Hard: Writing About Reading (Form 6)
- Getting-to-Know-You Interview (Form 7)*

Forms to Help You Gauge Students' Reading Levels at the Beginning of the Year

- Reading Strategy Checklist (Form 8)
- Oral Reading Miscue Code (Form 9)
- Retelling: Procedure for Using as Assessment (Form 10)
- Retelling: Fiction (Form 11)
- Retelling: Nonfiction (Form 12)
- Reading Checklist: Behaviors and Attitudes (Form 13)
- Estimating Instructional Reading Levels at the Beginning of the Year (Forms 14 and 14A)*
- Evaluating Student Assessments (Form 15)*
- Planning Form for Documenting Response to Intervention (Form 16)*
- Strategic Reading Conference (Form 17)

* The forms are customizable on the CD.

and directions. The chapter ends with a chart that spotlights student behaviors you might observe during these opening weeks of school and offers scaffolding and reteaching suggestions, ideas for professional study, and the closing "Continue to Reflect and Wonder . . ." that encourages reflection and questioning.

Estimate Students' Instructional Reading Levels and Identify Interests and Attitudes Toward Reading

During late August or early September, when you're at school arranging your classroom and attending meetings, set aside time to review students' folders filed in the school office. First, read the folders of students who have transferred and are new to your school system. Look for clues in the comments and notes made by the previous year's teacher. Study all the standardized test scores for reading comprehension and vocabulary and look for patterns:

◆ Are the scores flat and not improving?

◆ Do the scores show an annual decline?

◆ Do you observe a steady, upward trend?

◆ Does the student make progress some years but not others?

◆ Who is consistently in the bottom quartile?

Next, make three columns. In one, list students whose scores improve annually. In the second, list students who are in the bottom quartile and show little to no forward movement. In the third, list students who you feel you need more data on before estimating where you'd place them. You can avoid this step, with the exception of transfer students, if your school sends data sheets that list students' names, their instructional reading levels based on state tests, and input from their previous teacher.

You can discuss any of these assessments, which you'll find on the CD, in a conference with a student, administrators, a literacy coach or reading resource teacher, and parents. Tell students that these assessments will not be graded, but will be used to support their learning. This encourages them to be open and honest.

Now you'll want to get to know your students' interests and attitudes toward reading as well as how they see their strengths and weaknesses. These assessment forms will give you additional insights into all students and determine which ones you'd like to hear read aloud to monitor their pattern of error and recall in a retelling.

I've listed a menu of forms on page 32 that you can choose from and a few samples to show you the kind of information you can gather to get to know your students. Remember, all of the forms are on the CD.

Eleven Questions About Reading

First show students how you respond to these questions so they can gain insights into your reading life and develop a mental model of what a detailed response looks like. I suggest that you answer three to four questions a day and place a question and your response on chart paper. This way students can use the chart as a resource when they work on their own responses. Have students work on these questions during independent reading and writing times. Encourage them to complete no more than two to three each day so they can write thoughtful comments.

I find that students are candid and honest as long as you explain that you need this information to help them. Here are some quotes from students in grades five to eight:

"I never read. It's boring. I'd rather play hoops." —eighth grader

"Maybe it [reading] can help your spelling. It hasn't done anything for me."
—sixth grader

"It [reading] makes me want to do something else." —fifth grader

"I haven't finished a book since second grade." —seventh grader

"I read because I go into other worlds." —eighth grader

"What are strategies?" —fifth grader

"My favorite author is Dr. Seuss." —eighth grader

"Avi, I read every book he writes." —seventh grader

Answers like these provide a rich array of topics to discuss with students during your first reading conference.

What's Easy? What's Hard?

You can focus these questions on independent or instructional reading or on any aspect of writing. Show students how you respond; they'll be surprised and pleased to learn that you find some reading a challenge. Students' responses frequently offer insights into how they see themselves as readers. In Figure 2.1, it's obvious that this sixth grader finds reading a chore and gets no pleasure from it. You'll find the statements students make excellent and useful topics for conferences. At our first conference, I asked Morgan what she meant by "Some books are easier than others."

"The words are always hard. Can't say them," she replied, anger and frustration in her voice. That was a clue to me that the grade-level material Morgan was reading was too difficult. My job now was to find her instructional reading level and offer her several suspense books (the topic she loved) that she could read and enjoy. My hope was that she would find an author she liked.

Name _MORGAN_____Date_ _ _ ___

WHAT'S EASY and WHY?

Some book are
easy because some
books are easyier
than others.

WHAT's HARD and WHY?

I haven't found
a good arther
yet.

Figure 2.1 Sixth grader's response to what's easy and what's hard about reading; see Form 5 on the CD

Interest Inventory

On the CD, you'll find one interest inventory for grades 4 to 5 (Form 3) and one for grades 6 and up (Form 4). Knowing students' interests means you can help them find reading materials they care about. You'll also learn how much television they watch, how much time they spend on the computer, what their attitude toward reading is, and what their favorite authors and genres are.

Reading Strategy Checklist

This checklist gives you insights into what students know about the three-part reading framework and which strategies they use before, during, and after reading. I like to ask students to complete the checklist during the first week of school, again in January, and then near the end of school. This way they can observe their progress, and I can gather data to discuss during a conference and to decide whether scaffolding is necessary. In Figure 2.2, you'll find fifth-grader Bobby's January checklist. (See Form 8 on the CD.) In September, Bobby indicated that the only strategy he had was previewing. When he compared his first and second checklist, Bobby observed that the best thing he learned was to self-monitor by asking questions and rereading to "get the meaning." He also felt that he was learning how to "get words he could say and didn't understand." When Bobby completed his third strategy checklist in May and compared it to the first two in a conference with me, he said, "I can help myself when I'm stuck and don't get the meaning." And that's the goal of our teaching and assessment—to improve students reading skill and stamina and move them toward independence!

A Reading Strategy Checklist

Name **Bobby**   Date **1-16**

Directions: Check those statements that reflect the strategies you use.

<u>Strategies I Use Before Reading</u>

- ☑ I think about the cover, title, and topic.
- ☑ I read the back cover and the print on the inside of the jacket.
- ☐ I ask questions.
- ☑ I predict.
- ☐ I skim the pictures, charts, graphs.
- ☑ I read headings and bold face type words.
- ☐ I think about what I know about the topic.

<u>Strategies I Use During Reading</u>

I can help me—I know what to do if I stuck.

- ☑ I stop and check to see if I understand what I'm reading.
- ☐ I make mental pictures.
- ☑ I identify confusing parts.
- ☑ I identify unfamiliar words.
- ☑ I reread to understand confusing parts and unfamiliar words
- ☑ I record an unfamiliar word that I can't figure out.
- ☐ I use pictures, graphs, charts to help me understand confusing parts.
- ☐ I stop and retell to check what I remember.
- ☐ I reread to remember more details.
- ☐ I read the captions under and above photographs, charts, graphs, etc.
- ☐ I predict and adjust as I read.
- ☐ I raise questions and read for answers.

<u>Strategies I Use After Reading</u>

- ☐ I think about why I liked it.
- ☑ I retell.
- ☐ I speak, draw, and/or write reactions.
- ☐ I reread favorite parts.
- ☐ I reread to find details.
- ☐ I picture characters and places and ideas.
- ☐ I predict what might happen to a character if the story continued.

Figure 2.2 A fifth grader documents his strategy use; see Form 8 on the CD

Reading Survey

This survey will give you insights into students' feelings about reading and books as well as what they know about strategies. You'll also learn whether students talk about their reading with peers and enjoy responding in journals about their reading. Encourage students to use separate paper so they can elaborate on their answers.

Quite often these reading surveys can give you insights into students' lives that can dramatically change how you view their reading lives. Take Mike, an eighth grader whose almost blank survey showed a student disengaged from reading. However, Mike chose to answer the first and fifth questions. For: *What words pop into your mind when you think of reading a book?* Mike wrote: "headache, BORING, not interested." For the fifth question, *Besides books, what other types of materials do you read?* Mike wrote this: "I read magazines about cars. I helped my dad rebuild the motor of our car. That got me into reading stuff like that. I try to find articles on the Internet about cars."

If Mike hadn't answered that question, I would have concluded that he was a disengaged reader who might struggle with grade-level material. I took Mike's two answers and reread them during our first conference. He grinned sheepishly when I said, "So there is stuff you like to read."

"Yeah," he replied, "but it's not school stuff."

Students like Mike don't want to be part of school reading and learning. Mike could read and understand his car magazines better than I could. He was very literate with material that captured his interest, but not in terms of the way schools define literacy. During the year, I helped Mike branch out to books and magazines about NASCAR racing, the Indy 500, and biographies about world-class car racers. Without the Reading Survey and other assessments, I would have misread Mike as a weak, disinterested reader. He did branch out into biographies and discovered he "liked to read about people I admire."

Getting-to-Know-You Conferences

To help students feel safe when you chat with them about their reading, hold these brief meetings in a quiet place away from other students. You can confer at a small table in your room. If your room is small, place two chairs outside the door and chat there; you'll be able to observe the class while you confer. Your goal is to encourage students to discuss their reading strengths and needs. Tell them that you need honest replies because you want to support them and help them progress. Remember, though, not every student will feel comfortable sharing the first time you meet. However, if you establish a trusting and safe class environment during the first weeks of school, you'll find conferring easier for you and them. One way trust develops is when teachers do not to assume students don't care, are disinterested, or are careless. Taking the time to meet with and listen to students is one way to build trust. Another strategy is to help students understand that surveys and getting-to-know-you conferences are ungraded; the purpose is for students to be honest so we can help them. When you praise their honesty, they will continue to offer feedback, and you will continue to build a trusting learning community.

Start a five- to six-minute conference by discussing the information you gathered from various assessments, such as the interest inventory and reading survey. Encouraging students to discuss and explain what they have written often results in further insights that will help you estimate their instructional reading levels. Invite students to share what they do well both in and out of school, and share your interests and personal reading life with them. Make sure you react positively to students' responses and praise their honesty. Explain that you need to know about their reading lives so you can support them. Knowing what students enjoy reading will help you recommend books and magazines that will engage them.

Accept in advance that some students will tell you "Reading is stupid," "Reading is dumb and boring," "Books suck," or "No one can make me read." It's important to move beyond these comments and the frustration they stir within you. This is the way struggling and reluctant readers transmit the message that they require help and need your support.

Oral Reading Error Analysis

Since this is time-consuming, I recommend that you do this only when you are unsure of a student's instructional level. First, choose the book that you feel is an instructional fit. Keep one book at a lower level and one at a higher level nearby, just in case you're off target. You can also use selections from basal readers at different grade levels.

1. Photocopy the two pages from each of the three texts that you plan to ask the student to read. Tell the student that you will mark the patterns of his or her reading on your photocopy.

2. Provide background information by offering a one- or two-sentence summary of the passage. Then help the student access prior knowledge and experience about the topic.

3. Have the student read the two pages aloud from the text you thought was at his or her instructional reading level. Listen for errors that can affect meaning, such as omitting a key word, or substituting or mispronouncing a word that changes the passage's meaning. Mark notes on the photo-copied pages.

4. Keep a copy of the Oral Reading Miscue Code nearby (see page 41 and Form 9 on the CD). Until you have done this many times and know the symbols, the key will help you.

5. Ask the student to reread the passage silently and let him know he will have to retell it. I do this because I have found that when students read orally, they're so focused on "saying" the words that they don't have adequate recall. Follow the guidelines for retelling a narrative or informational text that's on the CD (Form 10). Retellings are a measure of readability because students can retell only what they understand. A rich retelling for fiction includes the main character's name, mention of other characters, plot details in sequence, and some personal connections. For nonfiction, retellings include specific details about the information in the text and some personal connections.

6. Choose three to five words and and ask the student to explain their meanings. Reread the sentence that contains each word. Many students in grades four and up experience comprehension problems because they have limited vocabularies and are unable to use context clues to figure out the meanings of unfamiliar words.

7. If the student's retelling has rich details, and if the student makes no more than five errors that affect meaning, then the level of the book is probably a good instructional choice. If the book is too hard, repeat the procedure with an easier text. If the book is too easy, use the more challenging text.

8. To score the passage, use the guidelines in the box on page 40.

What to Look for in Retellings

When students retell a passage, you gain insight into their recall and comprehension skills. To retell, the student must synthesize the text into his or her own words, then organize and order details.

Open with: *Take your time and think about the passage. Jot down notes if that will help you retell everything you remember. I will jot down what you're saying so I have a record of the retelling.*

After the student stops, if you feel the retelling needs more details, ask, *Can you recall more details? Would you like to add anything?* (If the student asks you to read back the retelling, do so, and note the request.)

Scoring the Passage

To interpret the oral reading error analysis, I use the criteria that Woods and Moe set in their Analytic Reading Inventory (1999). For a quick comprehension assessment, I have students retell the passage after they reread it silently.

I've included the three reading levels to help you decide whether a passage was too easy, too difficult, or "just right."

Instructional Reading Level: Student makes no more than three errors in 100 words, and the retelling reveals comprehension and recall of about 75 percent of the passage.

Independent Reading Level: Student makes no more than one error in 100 words and offers a detailed retelling of the passage that shows about 90 percent recall and comprehension. Sometimes a student might retell the passage in great detail and make two to three errors. Use your judgment and knowledge about the student to decide whether or not the student can read at this level with confidence and pleasure.

Frustration Reading Level: The book is too difficult because the student makes six or more miscues per 100 words and can retell few details.

Questions and Prompts to Help You Interpret an Oral Reading and Retelling

Having questions and prompts that guide your thinking about a student's oral reading and retelling can assist you in scoring and interpreting the results.

- ◆ List strong points of retelling.
- ◆ Did the student read through punctuation? How did this affect the retelling?
- ◆ Was the retelling rich in details?
- ◆ Was the student able to explain the vocabulary?
- ◆ Did the student read with expression that showed understanding?
- ◆ Did you have to change the selection used? Explain.
- ◆ Did the student make comments about the reading? About himself or herself as a reader?

Tell your classes that you are estimating students' instructional reading levels and that you could be off target. Ask students to tell you if a book they've chosen is too hard or if they don't connect to the book. Encourage students to discuss changing a book after reading the first two to three chapters. As Spencer, an eighth grader, notes, "A boring 100-page book is harder to read than a 300-page book you love."

- ◆ How many errors truly affected meaning and comprehension?
- ◆ What was the student's instructional level based on this assessment?

Oral Reading Miscue Code

This is the code from Mary Lynn Woods' and Alden J. Moe's *Analytical Reading Inventory*, Saddle River, NJ: Merrill, 1999, sixth edition.

THE FOUR MISCUES THAT FOLLOW ARE COUNTED AS ERRORS.

Code	Meaning	Example
O	Omitted word. Circle the word.	A loud (explosion) caused the fire in the old house.
I	Insertion. Write inserted word or words.	Flames spewed big ^sparks that destroyed other buildings.
S	Substitution. Write the substitution which can be a real word or nonword.	The moose stood silently in the grass meadow, watching the prey.
A	Aided word. Draw a diagonal through the word you helped student pronounce.	The therapeutic dose was taken every four hours.

THE FOUR MISCUES THAT FOLLOW ARE NOT COUNTED AS ERRORS.

Code	Meaning	Example
Rp	Repetition. Underline the repeated words. If repeated more than once, underline for each repetition.	<u>The coyote tensed</u> its muscles before leaping on the <u>unsuspecting</u> rabbit.
SC	Self-corrected. Readers often repeat a word or phrase or pause and use semantic or context clues to self-correct.	home SC The house is near the mall. SC Mud (spattered) her new tricycle.
/	Hesitates. If a student reads haltingly, making many hesitations, mark those, for it indicates a lack of fluency.	During the/circus,/the monkeys jumped/from horse to horse while/ dogs did/cartwheels/on the mat.
X	Ignores punctuation. Use the x for punctuation within a sentence or when they ignore end of sentence punctuation. This indicates they are not monitoring meaning.	Sitting by the fire x the old dog yawned and scratched his neck. x Suddenly, the cat, sitting nearby x leaped on the dog's back.

Interpreting Assessments You Gather at the Start of the Year

I set up a file folder for each student to store the assessments I gather throughout the year. After I review a set of assessments, I staple or clip them together with my estimated instructional reading level on top. I store these folders in plastic crates, in a file cabinet, or on a shelf in a closet.

Here's what goes into each student's literacy assessment folder for the first round of assessments:

- a note about their performance on standardized tests; jot down the percentile and the quartile for reading comprehension and vocabulary on a sheet of paper (some states, like Texas, give teachers a Lexile level based on students' performance on their state reading test);
- one completed getting-to-know you conference form (Form 7 on the CD);
- two to three other assessments; and
- an oral reading error analysis, if it was needed.

I use the questions and prompts in the next section to estimate each student's reading level. The steps to this process are also on Form 14 on the CD; you can record your responses on Form 14A.

Estimating Instructional Reading Level at the Beginning of the Year

Review artifacts in the literacy folder.
Note student's interests.

- What are the student's hobbies?
- What does the student do in his or her spare time?
- Any favorite genres? authors? movies? videos?
- What does the student do on the computer?

Note student's reading strengths.

- What books does the student enjoy reading?
- What strategies does the student understand?
- Can the student self-monitor?
- Does the student have and use fix-up strategies?
- Does the student read outside of school? Give examples.

- How does the student see himself or herself as a reader?
- What is the student presently reading?

Add notes/comments from the previous year's teacher.

- What are the student's strengths?
- What instructional book did the student read at the end of the year?
- Did the teacher feel that this instructional book was a good match?
- Did the teacher note ways this student learns best?
- Were there any needs pointed out?

Review results of oral reading error analysis and retelling, if applicable.

- Use the instructional reading level you arrived at using the questions and prompts on pages 40–42.

Estimated instructional reading level.

- Based on all the evidence reviewed, estimate the student's instructional reading level.

Estimating Instructional Reading Levels After Completing Your First Unit

Once you've completed a first round of differentiated whole-class reading instruction, you'll need to think about adjusting students' instructional reading levels for the second unit, which can be a repeat of whole-class differentiation or small group instruction. To accomplish this, you'll need to review and evaluate each student's progress using:

- journal entries;
- observational notes (see pages 44–46);
- other assessments, such as tests, projects, oral presentations; and
- observations made during conferences or small group meetings.

The decisions you make will depend on each student's ability to:

- show you their knowledge and application of practiced reading strategies;
- use details from a text to support inferences and answer interpretive questions;
- use context clues to figure out the meanings of unfamiliar words;
- write about their reading;
- participate in paired and group discussions; and
- show you process during one-on-one conferences.

Once you've reviewed this information, you can decide whether a student can stretch to a higher instructional level or whether staying at the same level would be more beneficial. I find that the observational notes I've taken during diverse learning situations support my decision making because I'm watching and jotting notes about a student's active learning and participation.

Taking Observational Notes

Learning to be a keen observer is an important aspect of assessment because we have notes that refresh our memories of student's learning habits and patterns. Taking notes on students while they work during class is crucial for middle and high school teachers who see more than 100 students each day because memories become fuzzy.

Finding the time to take observational notes in addition to planning lessons, grading papers, teaching, and attending meetings can feel overwhelming, especially if you have never done this type of assessing. *Start small.* Set aside five to ten minutes twice a week and observe one student at a time. Once you feel at ease with the process, try two, then three, and even four. With three to four students, you'll have to tag on an extra day for observing and an additional five minutes each day.

To ensure success, it's important to explain to students what you're doing and how it can benefit their reading skills. I also let students read the notes I wrote if they want to, or I tell them they will read the notes during a conference. It's important to prevent students from thinking that you're jotting down negatives. Remember how you feel when an administrator observes you and writes furiously the entire time. Immediately, you think that something's wrong.

Here are the three observational notes I took on sixth grader Edward (a pseudonym) during the first week of our reading-writing workshop (see Figure 2.3). The reason I focused on Edward is that I noticed issues with partner work and listening to mini-lessons. These notes were my rationale for holding a conference with Edward instead of waiting until the third week, when I would have had more data on him and all my students. The notes point to disengagement with the work,

Edward 9/8

Edward read his book during the entire lesson. He kept the book in his desk.

Edward 9/11

Edward listened to his partner but did not share. This happened 3X. His partner asked to change to a new partner.

Edward 9/12

Doesn't want to work with a group or partner. Says, "I like to do things myself."

Figure 2.3 *My observational notes on a sixth grader who seemed disengaged early in the year*

an unwillingness to work with a peer, and an intense interest in independent reading, even during my lessons. Edward, who came to my school in fourth grade, explained during our conference that his classmates disliked him and made fun of his curly hair and reading habits. He preferred to work alone, he told me, and read while I was teaching because, in Edward's words, "I like reading better than listening."

Working with and supporting Edward was a challenge. I tried several strategies, including asking him to pilot working with a partner, and giving him extra reading time when he showed me he completed work early. There are no pat answers for situations like this. It's a matter of continually trying another approach if the current one doesn't work.

Be Objective and Avoid Editorializing

Work hard to avoid making judgmental statements such as "Theresa dislikes reading," "Mandy enjoys disrupting her group," or "Mike has no pride in his work; it's always sloppy."

Instead, write only what you see. The above notes can be rewritten this way: "Theresa thumbs through magazines and chooses books that are too difficult." "When Mandy's group works silently or quietly, she tells a joke, talks about her favorite TV show, or asks questions." "Mike's journal has more doodles than writing about reading. Mike's writing is tough to read—Mike has trouble reading an entry to me."

Think about the tips that follow as you begin this type of assessment. Remember, to avoid escalating anxiety and frustration, start small and watch only one student until *you feel ready* to add another to observe.

Guidelines to Help You Take Observational Notes

Here are some situations that you can choose to observe students: paired or small-group discussions, silent reading, journal work, collaborative projects, choosing a book from the class library, completing a reading log, and taking a test or quiz.

◆ Jot down objective notes about a student's behavior and actions in different learning situations.

Observational Note-Taking Management Tip

Each day that I plan to take observational notes, I prepare a clipboard by placing four to six sticky notes on a blank piece of paper on the clipboard. If you plan to observe one student in several different situations, date each sticky note, and place the student's name at top. If you plan to observe two to three students, place their names and the date at the top of the sticky note. Before you observe, jot down the situation.

Carry a pencil and extra sticky notes with you or store them close by so they're accessible. I like to thread braided wool through the clip at the top of the board and wear it like a shoulder bag. This way I don't put it down and forget where I placed it.

When you have a free moment, place the notes on a blank sheet of paper and file in the student's literacy assessment folder. Use these notes in one-on-one conferences.

- Writing your notes may occur *after* an observed situation. For example, you will jot down notes after you meet with a reading group, with a pair of students, or support a collaborative project.

- Share observations with students because this enables you to raise their awareness of what they can do to move forward. Observations can be about learning situations or about students' behaviors during these situations. State what you notice and avoid an accusatory tone of voice. Invite students to respond. Do this during a short conference and ask the student to set a reasonable and reachable goal.

- Reread these notes and use them as you evaluate a set of assessments, then adjust your instructional plans and create scaffolds.

Professional Development Suggestions

When to Take Observational Notes

You can observe students in any situation at school, then jot down notes about what you've seen and heard. Watch students while you read aloud or present lessons; while they read, work with a partner or small group, discuss material, collaborate on a group project, or make a presentation; and during recess and lunch if you are with your class at those times. Remember, the goal is to gather information that deepens your insights into a child's behavior while learning and interacting—and always with the goal of supporting that child.

When middle school students struggle in one class, it's helpful to observe these same students in other subjects. Sometimes the problem exists in other classes, other times in one class. This data enables grade-level teams to pool their expertise to support a student.

Teachers and I find it helpful to share and review assessments and data we've gathered during these first weeks of school at team or faculty meetings. Gathering feedback on questions you have from colleagues can help you view a perceived problem from a new perspective. For example, an English teacher brought this student issue that arose from an interest survey to a sixth-grade team meeting: Larry, a sixth grader, wrote that he had no interests. He watched television all afternoon and evening. He found reading useless and boring and did not complete any summer reading. The teacher, starting her second year, didn't know how to handle the situation. Based on her own educational experiences, she would have given Larry an F for not completing summer reading and a second F for not presenting a book talk on summer reading. The group agreed that two failing grades would only add to Larry's frustration and anger and turn him further away from reading.

We suggested two things as starting points. The first was to administer an oral reading error analysis (see page 38). The second was to find out what Larry watched on television, which programs or sports events he enjoyed, and compliment him on his honesty. Larry's name came up frequently at team meetings, and we all provided feedback geared at building self-confidence and ensuring that Larry had some successful learning experiences to build on at school.

In addition to sharing assessments with colleagues and seeking feedback from them, it's important to read what other educators have to say about assessment and taking observational notes. In the box at right are some professional materials teams can read and discuss—materials that will fine tune their understanding of assessment in the differentiated classroom and how it drives your instructional decisions.

> *Professional Books to Dip Into and Discuss*
>
> • *Collaborative Analysis of Student Work: Improving Teaching and Learning* by Langer, Cotton, & Goff, ASCD, 2003.
>
> • *Differentiating Reading Instruction: How to Teach Reading to Meet the Needs of Each Student* by Laura Robb, Scholastic, 2008.
>
> • *Reading Assessment*, 2nd edition by JoAnne Schudt Caldwell, Ph.D., Guilford, 2008.
>
> • *Taking Note: Improving Your Observational Note Taking* by Brenda Miller Power, Stenhouse, 1996.

Scaffolding and Reteaching Chart for the Opening Weeks of School

Watch students while you read aloud for fun, while you deliver an instructional read aloud, when students pair-share or engage in whole-class discussions, when they complete journal work, and when they read silently. As you note your observations and reflect on them, you may notice areas in which individuals or groups need extra support. The chart below offers reteaching and scaffolding suggestions for some of the common areas that arise in the first weeks of school.

Assessment	Student Behavior	Scaffolding and Reteaching
Choosing an independent reading book	• Selects books that are too difficult. • Takes an overly long amount of time to choose a book. • Takes several books without looking them over.	• Confer to discover interests and/or use student's interest survey. • Have student work with a classmate to choose books. • Suggest several books for student to choose from. • Help student practice how to decide if materials are readable.
Observations of independent reading	• Has difficulty settling down to read. • Chats during silent reading times. • Goes to the bathroom two to three times during silent reading. • Leafs through materials but avoids reading.	• Confer to find out why the student has difficulty settling down to read. • Make sure that the student has the background knowledge to understand selected reading materials. • Find computer games with text that interests the student and start there. • Offer the student magazines that relate to his or her interests.
Observations of whole-class discussions	• Does not raise hand and participate. • Doodles during this time. • Does not answer after pair-shares. • Does work for other classes.	• Confer to find out why the student is not participating. • Ask what you, the teacher, can do to help the student feel comfortable participating. • Prepare student for responding to a question you will pose so that you build self-confidence.

continued . . .

Assessment	Student Behavior	Scaffolding and Reteaching
Observations during teacher read-aloud	• Appears inattentive. • Does homework. • Tries to chat with a classmate. • Avoids writing in journal or writes very little. • Doesn't volunteer to read journal response. • Does not look at journal when he or she volunteers to read. • Says much more than is written in the journal.	• Confer to find out why the student appears inattentive or is doing other work. Negotiate ways to support the student, such as move student closer to you; periodically explain your homework policy to the class; explain how your read-alouds include modeling and instruction; ask how you can help the student listen better. • Use scaffolds for student's journal writing, such as reviewing how to set up the journal page and showing how you look back in the text to gather details. • Ask student to tell you the ideas for a journal entry. Jot some of these down in the student's journal then gradually turn the writing over to the student. • Ask student to read what he or she has written and discuss the entry. Encourage the student to elaborate his or her ideas.
Observations of behavior during mini-lessons	• Appears inattentive. • Does not participate in collaborations. • Does not ask questions about the lesson. • Says these are "boring."	• Confer to see whether student is listening, for appearances are not always accurate. • Find out if the student has enough background knowledge to connect to the mini-lesson. If not, help the student build background knowledge. • Work one-on-one. Some learners need to hear the lesson with the teacher sitting nearby. • Confer to discover why the student doesn't add to collaborations or pose questions. Then set up a situation where you prepare the student to suggest an idea before the lesson. If self-confidence is an issue, this can help.
Observations during first conferences	• Avoids eye contact. • Fidgets and appears nervous. • Does not offer helpful or meaningful answers.	• Use data gathered from assessments the student completed to start the conversation. • Assure the student that you want to support and help him or her by conferring. • Tell student that you will reschedule the conference. • Invite the student to talk to peers who have enjoyed the conference with you.

Continue to Reflect and Wonder . . .

What you model, the routines you teach, and the assessments you gather the first weeks of school or prior to initiating a whole-class differentiated unit create a positive tone, a safe and trusting class culture, and a sense of community. Use the questions below to reflect on the importance of getting to know your students and establishing learning routines.

◆ What have I learned from other teachers about specific students' learning needs?

◆ How am I pacing myself with new assessment practices?

◆ Why is it helpful to work with a colleague to discuss new practices and feelings about change?

◆ How am I communicating to students that I'm taking observational notes?

◆ How do I use observational notes?

◆ How am I building students' self-confidence during our first conference?

CHAPTER 3

Assessment Forms for Reading Strategy Conferences

*I*n a district not too far from Winchester, Virginia, where I live, teachers in grades four and up use a grading system mandated by the district. Teachers arrive at a grade by finding the average of students' tests, quizzes, written work, worksheets, and homework. Items are weighted so that tests count more than quizzes, with homework counting the least amount. The purpose of this system is to objectively arrive at a grade. This grading system reduces children to a set of numbers, and paces teachers so they "cover" the curriculum students need to know for the annual state tests without addressing the progress or lack of progress among students. Grades and covering material is what this assessment system is all about. Holding a conference to find out why a student fails or doesn't understand, then intervening to support the student, is not a consideration here.

Recently, a telephone call from a parent of a first grader in this system led me to conclude that this grading system had trickled down to first grade. The parent asked for help because out of twenty-five first-grade students, fourteen were failing, including her son. Instead of reflecting on the needs of each student, the teacher met the district's pacing goals and marched through the curriculum without considering that children who didn't "get it" the first time around can and should be helped. It's sad to see the cycle of student failure and low self-esteem develop as early as first grade. The parent who called me hired a tutor to help her son pass first grade and maintain some self-confidence. However, not every parent could afford a tutor, so a large number of first graders failed.

Assessment used only to give a grade is not what assessment for differentiating reading instruction is all about. Assessment in the differentiated reading classroom or even in a more traditional classroom should consider the whole student—behavior, oral and written work, paired and group interactions—and use this data to confer with students and explore ways to support each one to help them improve and steadily move forward. Over time, such responsive teaching will improve reading test scores.

Reading strategy conferences are a key part of this type of assessment, and the forms in this chapter will give you a window into each student's thinking as they apply strategies in a conference setting.

As You Continue to Read . . .

You'll want to make sure that the observational notes you collect (see pages 44–46) include situations that are part of the three-part framework of before, during, and after reading. In addition to written work, you'll also have notes to discuss at conferences.

First you'll review a chart of assessments that help you document conferences that examine how students apply strategies before, during, and after reading. So you can gain insights into how I document and interpret these assessments, I analyze a conference held on a strategy from each part of the framework; forms that assess other strategies and skills are on the CD. The chapter ends with a chart that spotlights student behaviors and offers scaffolding and reteaching suggestions, ideas for professional study, and the closing "Continue to Reflect and Wonder . . ."

Assessing in the Three-Part Reading and Learning Framework

The three-part reading framework offers a manageable, logical way to organize and assess reading strategy instruction. It breaks learning down into distinct stages, each with its own purpose. Before reading, students activate prior knowledge, preview texts, explore new vocabulary, and engage in other activities that prepare them to read. During reading, students learn to monitor their comprehension and repair it with fix-up strategies when it falters. After reading, students reflect on their reading through discussions and writing in order to construct

Definitions of Strategies in the Three-Part Framework

In Appendix A (pages 135–137), you'll find a chart that lists and gives a short explanation of each before, during, and after reading strategy included in this chapter.

Forms for Chapter 3
That You'll Find on the CD

Before-Reading Assessment Forms

- Checklist of Strategies Students Use Before Reading (Form 18)

Conference Forms for

- Preview and Set Purposes (Form 19)
- Preview/Connect/Predict (Form 20)
- Preview/Question (Form 21)
- List/Group/Label (Form 22)
- Fast Write (Form 23)

During-Reading Assessment Forms

- Checklist of Strategies Students Use During Reading (Form 24)
- Checklist for Monitoring Independent Reading (Form 25)

Conference Forms for

- Predict/Support/Confirm/Adjust (Form 26)
- Read/Pause/Retell (Form 27)
- INSERT (Form 28)
- Queries for Questioning the Author (Form 29)
- Questioning the Author with Fictional Texts (Form 30)
- Questioning the Author with Informational Texts (Form 31)
- Reread and Close Read (Form 32)
- Visualizing (Form 33)
- Building Vocabulary Using Context Clues (Form 34)
- Making Connections (Form 35)

After-Reading Assessment Forms

- Checklist of Strategies Students Use After Reading (Form 36)

Conference Forms for

- Making Inferences About Characters or People (Form 37)
- Determining Importance (Form 38)
- Making Connections (Form 39)
- Synthesizing Information (Form 40)
- Vocabulary Strategy Growth (Form 41)
- Questioning (Form 42)

new understandings, make connections, and explore big ideas. Using this research-tested framework slows down the learning and encourages self-monitoring and reflection. It offers students ways to unpack meaning in challenging texts, to create new understandings, and to connect ideas and concepts (Dowhower, 1999; Gillet & Temple, 2000; Robb, 2000; Tierney & Readence, 2000; Vaughan & Estes, 1986).

The three-part reading chart on page 51 lists the forms you'll find on the CD—forms that assess key strategies you and I present in our language arts classes. I've taken one form from each part of the framework and shown how I use each one to gain insight into students' application of strategies and infer their needs.

In the next section, you'll explore one conference from each part of the framework that I complete with students.

Conference Snapshots: Before, During, and After Reading

"Why are reading strategy conferences essential?"

"How do I confer about a strategy in only five minutes?"

"How often should I conduct a reading strategy conference?"

These are typical questions I receive from teachers when I introduce conferences as a key aspect of instruction when differentiating reading lessons. During a conference teachers can check:

◆ students' understanding of how to apply a strategy;

◆ how the strategy supports reading comprehension;

◆ whether students can successfully apply a strategy;

◆ if scaffolding the learning is improving students' understanding;

◆ whether students are ready for gradual release with the strategy; and

◆ whether reteaching will support students' understanding and application of a strategy.

This list illustrates how conferring becomes a key instructional tool when teachers differentiate with whole-class genre/issue studies. (See Chapter 4 in my book *Differentiating Reading Instruction*, 2008a.) As you read on, I will address the question of managing time and how many students to confer with each day.

Management Tips and Conference Goals

One of the first tips I offer teachers when they start holding conferences on strategies (or any topic) is to be a good listener. Once you've asked a question, count to 100 before you say anything. Students need time to think and collect their thoughts. Avoid prompting them so they are aware of what you want them to say. This is tough to do, but essential if you want to encourage students to talk. Consider excerpts from two conferences. In the first, I ask a fifth grader to reread a journal entry where she was asked to draw conclusions about a character's personality and offer support from her book. In the second example, I invite a sixth grader to explain how he determines importance.

First Example:

Robb: Can you tell me more about this journal entry?

Student: (*Shrugs her shoulders. Says nothing. I count to 100, then ask a question.*)

Robb: Can you give me an example of a personality trait?

Student: Not sure what that is.

Robb's Reflections: *By waiting and resisting the desire to point out that the student described physical traits such as hair and height, the girl was able to tell me that she did not know what personality traits were. Now I can help this student understand the difference between a physical trait and a personality trait, because she has recognized this need. Once she gets that, I can reteach how to use what characters say, do, think, and decide to figure out their personalities.*

Second Example:

Robb: Can you tell me how you determine the important details?

Student: I just do it.

Robb: Can you explain what's happening when you do it?

Student: Ummm. (*No answer.*)

Robb: Let's look at the strategy chart. (*My goal is for the student to review the chart to see if it jogs his memory.*)

Student: It says you set purposes first.

Robb: How do you do that?

Student: Well . . . you read it.

Robb's Reflections: *It appears that this sixth grader has not absorbed the strategy because he cannot explain how it works. This short conference lets me know that this student (along with three others) needs reteaching and additional practice.*

Focus conferences on one aspect of a strategy so they last from four to five minutes. Know your focus in advance, as this saves time. Share your focus with the student, since this helps students collect their thoughts and raise questions.

Less experienced teachers will feel comfortable conferring with two students each day class meets. Veterans will be able to complete four conferences a day, four times a week. This means that every three weeks, you can definitely meet with students who are reading below grade level and hold some follow-up conferences. You can meet with students reading at or above grade level at least once or twice a semester. You can also learn about this group's application of a strategy through self-evaluations (see Chapter 6).

Now, I invite you to study the conferences I documented with a fifth grader, a sixth grader, and an eighth grader.

One-On-One Conferences in Action

As soon as I've completed surveys and getting-to-know-you conferences, I confer with students reading below grade level because I want to gain insights into their strengths and needs. Doing this early in a differentiated unit of study enables me to create scaffolds and develop teaching and reteaching plans that can hopefully maximize their progress. I set the stage for each conference by giving some background information on the student (all names are pseudonyms) and my rationale for calling the conference.

Before-Reading Strategy Conference With Carlos

Carlos is a sixth grader whose instructional reading level is high third grade. His interest survey revealed a love of playing basketball with his buddies after school and presenting magic shows for his younger siblings. Tall for his age, Carlos is fast and has many basketball moves. He hopes to make the high school basketball team in three years. Carlos's responses to the eleven questions about reading (see Form 2 on the CD) contained several important points. He wrote, "I don't know strategies," and "I hate to read 'cause it's boring." Carlos underlines *boring* four times. His favorite author is R.L. Stine—only when the teacher reads the stories. Carlos wrote that when he reads, it always "feels like a LONG one." During our first conference, Carlos told me that he wrote LONG in caps because it took forever to read a page for any subject.

(And rightly so, as all of Carlos's texts were three years above his instructional reading level.) He also told me that he learned magic tricks by reading how to do them and then practicing. However, Carlos did not consider this reading. When asked why, Carlos answered, "It's not school stuff; it's what I like to do." This comment led me to conclude that Carlos will read material when he's motivated.

Our differentiated unit on biography started with a four-week mini-study using short chapter books. Carlos was reading *Harry Houdini: Master of Magic* by Robert Kraske. Students practiced previewing their books and raising questions. Carlos listened intently as I modeled the strategy in think-alouds with picture book biographies. The strategy chart (see model on page 55) hung on the chalkboard as a reference and resource for students.

Matching Books to Students

To find books that match students' instructional levels, use your school and classroom library. If your middle school does not have books you need, check out some from an elementary school in your district. However, school and class libraries should house collections of diverse genres that are below, at, and above specific grade levels.

What follows are my reasons for the first reading strategy conference:

1. Carlos felt he did not have any reading strategies.

2. Carlos read three years below grade level.

3. Carlos had negative feelings about reading at school.

4. Carlos had difficulty turning preview information into questions when I read aloud, modeled, and invited students to pair-share and suggest questions. Carlos was a listener in the pair-share experiences.

5. Carlos read to learn magic tricks. I wanted him to transfer his self-efficacy in that context to school reading and learning.

Focus of Conference: Start the Preview/Question With Carlos

I decided to model the Preview/Question strategy with Carlos before setting him to work independently so that he could observe my thinking closely, practice in front of me, and then experience success with this strategy. You'll find the form I completed based on my meeting with Carlos in Figure 3.1. (There's a reproducible version of Form 21 on the CD and on page 57.) I started the conference by modeling the Preview/Question strategy using *Shark Lady* by Ann McGovern. My rationale for doing this was to provide maximum support and give Carlos a positive experience that would boost his self-confidence with a doable strategy. Note that I decided to schedule a second conference so I would have another opportunity to say positive things to Carlos about his application of this strategy.

Preview/Question
A Before-Reading Strategy

WHAT
• A strategy that prepares you for reading

WHY
• Builds background knowledge
• Introduces vocabulary
• Starts thinking process with connections
• Encourages you to use information to raise questions
• Engages you in reading as you read on to discover answers to your questions

WHEN
• Nonfiction books, magazines, textbooks, newspapers

HOW
• Read bold face title, headings, words
• Study cover illustration
• Read captions
• Read maps, graphs, study pictures
• Connect information to what you know
• Use the title, illustrations, chapter titles, captions to pose questions

Name _Carlos_   **Date** _2/15_

Conference Form for Preview/Question

Directions:

1. Use the checklist below and any observational notes and student's written work as a guide for this conference.

2. Use a fiction or nonfiction text at the student's instructional reading level.

Before-Reading Strategy: Preview/Question

✓ The student can explain how to preview fiction or nonfiction texts.

___ The teacher modeled how to apply the strategy. _Used Shark Lady by Ann McGovern_

✓ The student previews using the title and cover.

✓ The student uses text features as part of the preview.

✓ The student uses chapter titles as part of the preview.

___ The student can create questions from information in the preview.

___ The student understands how preview/question supports reading comprehension.

Notes About the Student's Application of Preview/Question

Carlos observed & noted how I turned the title and cover illustration into questions. He successfully previewed & posed questions with title, cover, Chapter 1 title of his book. I watched Carlos Preview/Question Chapter 2. He said "I can do this." Told me that questions made him want to read. Grinned when I complimented his use of this strategy.

Check one of the statements:

___ Needs more support

✓ Can work independently
Decided on a follow-up to build self-confidence.

Set times for follow-up conferences: _2/20_

Additional Comments:

Figure 3.1 My reading strategy conference with Carlos; see Form 21 on the CD and a reproducible version on page 57

Student's Name _____ Date _____

Conference Form for Preview/Question

Directions:

1. Use the checklist below as well as observational notes and the student's written work, as a guide for this conference.

2. Use a fiction or nonfiction text at the student's instructional reading level.

BEFORE READING STRATEGY: PREVIEW/QUESTION:

_____ The student can explain how to preview fiction or nonfiction texts.

_____ The teacher modeled how to apply the strategy during the conference.

_____ The student previews fiction using the title, front and back covers, and part of first chapter.

_____ The student uses chapter and section titles and bold-faced vocabulary as part of the preview.

_____ The student uses nonfiction text features as part of the preview.

_____ The student can create questions from information in the preview.

_____ The student understands how Preview/Question supports reading comprehension.

NOTES ABOUT THE STUDENT'S APPLICATION OF PREVIEW/QUESTION:

Check one of the statements: _____ Needs more support _____ Can work independently

Set times for follow-up conferences:

ADDITIONAL COMMENTS:

During-Reading Strategy Conference With David

David is a fifth grader who was reading grade level texts at the end of fourth grade. When his teacher listened to David and his partner read a section of an article on rain forests, David could retell two details. David's teacher showed me a recent oral reading error analysis she'd completed with him.

We both noticed one key issue—David ignored words and phrases that he did not understand. He was an excellent decoder, but he was not monitoring his comprehension. We taught David and his classmates how to use INSERT, an acronym for Interactive Notation System for Effective Reading and Thinking (Vaughan & Estes, 1986). We introduced two notations—a check for "I understand" and a question mark for "I'm confused." In addition, we taught David and others in his group two fix-up strategies: reread and close read. Close read asks students to return to the words and phrases that confused them and try to make connections to what they know, explore context clues to figure out the meaning of tough words, connect the confusing part to what you already understand from the passage, or make sure you understand pronoun references. Twice a week, David's teacher or I pulled the small group together to practice using INSERT and accessing a fix-up strategy. We discovered that David and two other classmates often read through end-of-sentence punctuation, which diminished comprehension. We worked on pausing and taking a breath at the end of sentences. After three weeks on group and independent practice, David's teacher and I decided it was time to confer with him and other group members on the use of the self-monitoring strategy we'd been practicing. Here are our reasons for calling this conference:

> You can scaffold any strategy conference by modeling the specific strategy with a think-aloud. The amount of modeling you do depends on how much support the student requires.

1. to observe whether David could identify what he does and does not understand with a new selection or a new section of his book that's at his instructional reading level;

2. to see if David uses a fix-up strategy to "unconfuse" himself;

3. to observe how David uses context clues to figure out tough vocabulary; and

4. to note whether David uses background knowledge to connect to information in the text—background knowledge he already has and background knowledge he's gained from the preview and reading.

Figure 3.2 shows the conference form I used to assess David's ability to monitor his understanding of short sections of text using INSERT and fix-up strategies. Note that David sees the benefits of not reading through punctuation. Instead of saying words, David is now reading for meaning. David finds rereading, a great and easy-to-apply strategy, helpful. He needs more practice using context clues to unlock the meaning of tough words.

Student Name _David_   Date _9/17_

Conference Form for INSERT and Fix-Up Strategies

Directions:

1. Use the checklist below and any observational notes and student's written work as a guide for this conference.

2. Use a fiction or nonfiction text at the student's instructinal reading level. Work with a passage the student hasn't already read.

Self-Monitoring Strategy: INSERT

✓ The student identifies what he or she understands. _Did this well._

✓ The student pinpoints vocabulary that's unfamiliar.

___ The student can identify phrases/sentences that confuse.

✓ The students can explain why he or she is confused.

Notes about the student's application of INSERT.

Vocabulary confused David. We practiced using context clues. David was not using clues or text features. He understood how this helps.

Fix-Up Strategies: Reread, Close Read, Context Clues

✓ The student can name and explain how (reread,) close read, and (context clues) help and improve understanding of passages and vocabulary while reading.

___ The student applies each strategy appropriately.

Notes about the student's application of these fix-up strategies.

David told me he rereads a lot now and it helps him understand and remember.

Check one of the statements:

✓ Needs more support _close read, context clues_   ___ Can work independently

Set times for follow-up conferences: _9/26_

Additional Comments: _David says that stopping at ends of sentences is helping him understand more._

Figure 3.2 My reading strategy conference with David; see Form 28 on the CD and a reproducible version on page 60

Student's Name _____ Date _____

Conference Form for INSERT

Directions:

1. Reread and review any observational notes, interpretations of reading inventories, and student's written work. Summarize your observations and assessments below, using the checklist as a guide.

2. Use a fiction or nonfiction text at the student's instructional reading level. Work with a passage the student hasn't already read.

SELF-MONITORING STRATEGY: INSERT

_____ The student identifies what he or she understands.

_____ The student pinpoints vocabulary that's unfamiliar.

_____ The student can identify phrases or sentences that are confusing.

_____ The student can explain why he or she is confused.

NOTES ABOUT THE STUDENT'S APPLICATION OF INSERT:

FIX-UP STRATEGIES: REREAD, CLOSE READ, CONTEXT CLUES:

_____ The student can name and explain how reread, close read, and context clues help and improve understanding of passages and vocabulary while reading.

_____ The student applies each strategy appropriately.

NOTES ABOUT THE STUDENT'S APPLICATION OF THESE FIX-UP STRATEGIES:

Check one of the statements: _____ Needs more support _____ Can work independently

Set times for follow-up conferences:

ADDITIONAL COMMENTS:

After-Reading Strategy Conference With Jenny

Jenny is an eighth grader who I tutored during her sixth-grade year because she was reading two years below grade level. In sixth grade, Jenny did not enjoy reading and almost never chose reading as an at-home activity. I divided Jenny's four-times-a-week tutoring sessions into 20 minutes of instruction and practice with me and 25 minutes of independent reading. At first, Jenny chose to read teen magazines. An avid rider, Jenny moved to books about horses and read every one at her independent reading level that was in the school library and my classroom library.

By eighth grade, Jenny had developed a personal reading life and did spend some time reading at home. Her interpretations of texts were literal, and Jenny (along with three other classmates) had difficulty making inferences about characters' personality traits. After four weeks of modeling how I infer a character's personality traits using a read-aloud, referring to the how-to strategy chart posted on the chalkboard, and having Jenny practice with her instructional text, I decided to confer with each one of the four students to check on their progress.

Here are my reasons for calling a conference with Jenny:

1. After working with Jenny and her three classmates, I felt that she was able to identify a character's personality traits and find supporting details in the text.

2. I wanted to check this out one-to-one before moving to inferring about setting and conflicts.

3. At times Jenny used the list of adjectives on a wall in our class to find a word that described a personality trait. Sometimes, if a word was not on the list, Jenny gave up thinking.

Figure 3.3 shows the conference form I used to assess Jenny's progress. Note that Jenny has difficulty using dialogue to draw conclusions about a character. Even when she uses the chart, Jenny is unsure about which adjective describes what the character is like. She also can't clearly explain that an inference is an unstated meaning based on the content of the dialogue. She tells me that she's like a detective but doesn't explain that the characters' words contain the clues for making an inference about them.

Student name _Jenny_____ Date _10/1_____

Conference Form for Making Inferences About Characters or People

Directions:

1. Use the checklist below and any observational notes and student's written work as a guide for this conference.

2. The student can explain what an inference Use a fictional text at the student's instructional level. Work with a passage the student has read. However, the student should not have practiced inferring with the passage.

Making Inferences About Characters'/People's Personality from (Fiction) and Biography *The Watson's Go to Birmingham 1963 by C. P. Curtis*

✓ The student can explain what making inferences with (fiction) or biography means.

✓ The student infers a character's (or person's) personality traits using dialogue.

___ The student uses characters' (people's) inner thoughts to make inferences.

___ The student uses characters' (people's) decisions to make inferences.

___ The student uses how characters (people) handle conflict and/or problems to infer.

___ The students uses the character's (person's) actions and/or interactions to infer.

___ The student uses other characters' (people's) reactions to make inferences about the main character (person).

Notes about the student's application of making inferences about personality traits.

Jenny still can't find the words to explain making inferences. She says, "I'm like a detective," but stops there. On pages 3–4 Jenny inferred that Dad was a tease. She could not find a trait for momma.

Check one of the statements:

✓ Needs more support   ___ Can work independently

Set times for follow-up conferences: _10/9, 10/15_

Additional Comments: _I feel that Jenny is close to being able to apply inferring to dealogue. In addition to 2 more short meetings, I'll pair her with Kate._

Figure 3.3 My reading strategy conference with Jenny; see Form 37 on the CD and a reproducible version on page 63

Student's Name _____ Date _____

Conference Form for Making Inferences About Characters or People

Directions:

1. Use the checklist below and any observational notes and student's written work as a guide for this conference.

2. Use a fictional text or biography at the student's instructional level. Work with a passage the student has read. However, the student should not have practiced inferring with the passage. Ask the student to reread the passage during the conference and then think-aloud while making an inference about a character.

MAKING INFERENCES ABOUT CHARACTERS'/PEOPLE'S PERSONALITY FROM FICTION AND BIOGRAPHY

_____ The student can explain what making inferences with fiction or biography means.

_____ The student infers a character's (or person's) personality traits using dialogue.

_____ The student uses characters' (people's) inner thoughts to make inferences.

_____ The student uses characters' (people's) decisions to make inferences.

_____ The student uses how characters (people) handle conflict and/or problems to make inferences.

_____ The student uses the character's (person's) actions and/or interactions to make inferences.

_____ The student uses other characters' (people's) reactions to make inferences about the main character (person).

NOTES ABOUT THE STUDENT'S APPLICATION OF MAKING INFERENCES ABOUT CHARACTERS OR PEOPLE:

Check one of the statements: _____ Needs more support _____ Can work independently

Set times for follow-up conferences:

ADDITIONAL COMMENTS:

Professional Development Suggestions

Conversations about the strategies in the three-part framework can grow out of your experiences as well as from professional books and journal articles (see box below). I encourage teachers to share strategy lessons and questions with colleagues during team or faculty meetings. Presenters bring their queries and/or charts and samples of students' writing to show how their students applied a strategy; they bring a range of student samples, from those who didn't get it to those who did. Of course, it's delightful to share successes and explain what made the lessons work for students, then ask colleagues to share their experiences with the strategy. It's equally beneficial, however, for teachers to bring lessons that derailed to a meeting. Doing this enables the teacher to receive feedback and suggestions from peers. Moreover, a colleague might have experienced a similar glitch but refrained from sharing.

At a meeting at the start of the year, a first-year teacher brought the following issue to her team. She explained that she understood how to preview informational texts that contained nonfiction features such as sidebars, photographs and captions, diagrams, and excerpts from diaries. Her question was, "How do you preview fiction—chapter books without illustrations?"

A veteran English teacher responded by first affirming the query and this novice teacher's understanding of previewing informational text. Then she explained that students should think about the title and the front-cover

Six Professional Books About Strategies in the Three-Part Framework

- *Building Background Knowledge for Academic Achievement: Research on What Works in Schools* by Richard Marzano, ASCD, 2004.

- *Mosaic of Thought* by Ellin Oliver Keene and Susan Zimmerman, 2nd edition, Heinemann, 2007.

- *Strategies That Work* by Stephanie Harvey and Anne Goudvis, Stenhouse, 2000.

- *Reading Strategies and Practices: A Compendium* by Robert Tierney and John Readence, Allyn and Bacon, 2000.

- *Teaching Reading: A Differentiated Approach* by Laura Robb, Scholastic, 2008

- *Teaching Reading in Middle School* by Laura Robb, Scholastic, 2000.

- *Teaching Reading in Social Studies, Science, and Math* by Laura Robb, Scholastic, 2003.

illustration, then read the inside jacket and back cover as well as the first page or two. With that information, students could predict the genre and provide enough details to raise questions that would drive the reading.

This kind of trusting, supportive atmosphere is crucial for the development of new teachers and for veterans who want to change and grow. Besides inquiry and sharing lessons, team and faculty meetings can focus on a professional article or part of a book. I recommend that teachers complete the reading during a team meeting—read for 30 minutes, and discuss the reading for 15 minutes. The focus of conversations should deal with the text's content and how teachers might use it or adapt it to their teaching styles and students' needs. I have found that completing the reading during the school day insures that everyone will do it. Reading professional texts as homework means that several will be unable to complete their assignment due to outside responsibilities such as caring for children or an elderly and ailing parent.

Scaffolding and Reteaching Chart for Three-Part Framework Strategies

I've divided the chart on pages 66–69 into four parts. The first part will discuss all the before-reading strategies under the heading of "Building Students' Prior Knowledge," for that is the purpose of each strategy.

For during-reading strategies, you'll find two sections. The first deals with self-monitoring and the second with fix-up strategies. Again, I've used these broad categories because the goal for each strategy is the same.

The strategies listed under "After Reading" will be discussed one at a time because even though all call for high-level thinking, each strategy differs. For example, Determining Importance asks students to use their purposes for reading to find key details, while Inferring invites students to use text details to discover unstated meanings.

After assessing students' reading strategy use in conferences and journal work, listening to their discussions, and observing their behaviors during independent reading, you may identify areas in which students need extra support. The chart that follows offers suggestions for scaffolding and reteaching reading strategy application.

Scaffolding and Reteaching Chart for Three-Part Framework Strategies

Before Reading: Building Students' Prior Knowledge

Strategy	Student Behaviors	Scaffolding and Reteaching
Activating Prior Knowledge	• Offers few ideas when brainstorming. • Can't categorize ideas. • Has little prior knowledge of the topic. • Has no prior knowledge of the topic. • Says material is boring. • Doesn't pose questions after preview. • Doesn't predict after preview. • Doesn't pose questions about the topic. • Doesn't participate in prereading experiences.	• Enlarge background knowledge with pictures, read-alouds, video clips, Internet, discussions, and photographs. • Use nonfiction text features such as titles, headings, sidebars, etc. to increase prior knowledge. • Think aloud and show how you use prior knowledge to predict and pose questions. • Model how you use prior knowledge to make connections. • Have one-on-one conferences to discuss background ideas and build student's prior knowledge. • Pair students and have them support one another with gaining background knowledge, posing questions, and making predictions. • Preteach key vocabulary. • Preteach key concepts. • Show how a graphic organizer can help students record what they are learning and support recall of information. • Meet with individuals and small groups to enlarge prior knowledge and model how prior knowledge supports comprehension.

During Reading: Self-Monitor to Know What You Do and Don't Understand

Strategy	Student Behaviors	Scaffolding and Reteaching
Self-Monitor Understanding and Recall	• Reads through punctuation. • Has difficulty retelling details. • Has little to no recall of information. • Can't write about the material. • Doesn't participate in discussions. • Lacks the vocabulary to read and understand. • Can't pronounce many key words. • Finds the material boring. • Does not read the material. • Puts head down on desk during class reading times. • Skips over tough words.	• Model with a think-aloud how to read and stop for punctuation. • Have student practice reading and pausing for punctuation. Discuss how this helps comprehension. • Meet one-on-one to determine if the material is too difficult. • Find an easier text on the same topic so the student can read, learn, and contribute. • Preteach key concepts and related vocabulary. • Model how to decode tough and unfamiliar words. Have student practice. • Model how Questioning the Author can help students improve understanding of challenging parts of texts. • Ask student, "How can I help you?" • Model how to use Read/Pause/Retell/Reread or Read On using small chunks of text so student can self-monitor with small amounts of information. • Explain why self-monitoring can improve recall and understanding.

During Reading: Fix-Up Words, Phrases, and Sentences That Confuse

Strategy	Student Behaviors	Scaffolding and Reteaching
Fix-Up Strategies	• Has no strategies for repairing comprehension. • Cannot explain the purpose of a fix-up strategy. • Says that there's too much to fix up. • Gives up on the work.	• Meet with the student to determine the level of support needed. • Have student place tough words on sticky notes, with page number and title of book. Provide teacher and/or peer support with figuring out meaning. • Teach students how to use context clues to figure out tough words. • Model, one by one, different fix-up strategies, each time explaining how the strategy helps improve understanding and recall. • Think aloud and read and summarize small chunks of text and show how you pinpoint and repair confusing parts. • Have student practice reading and summarizing to test whether it's necessary to access a fix-up strategy. • Help students understand the benefits of each fix-up strategy.

After Reading: Think With Details to Create New Understandings

Strategy	Student Behaviors	Scaffolding and Reteaching
Inferring With Fiction and Biography	• Can't explain what inferring entails. • Finds literal meanings. • Can't use dialogue to infer. • Doesn't create mental images. • Has difficulty inferring with setting. • Has difficulty inferring with conflicts and problems. • Has difficulty inferring with character's thoughts, actions, and interactions. • Has difficulty using details to find themes. • Has trouble making personal connections. • Doesn't bring what he or she knows to the inferring process.	• Through your own think-alouds, help student understand that inferences are unstated or implied meanings. • Model how you infer, using one of these narrative elements at a time: setting, dialogue, actions, interactions, plot, inner thoughts, conflicts, decisions, problems. • Confer with student. Model, then have student practice in front of you. • Gradually release the inferring to the student. • Study author tags in dialogue, such as *shouted, wept, muttered.* • Model how you imagine the character's tone of voice and use this to infer feelings. • Help students visualize a character's expression and gestures and use these images to infer. • Explain that a theme is a general idea that the author explores through characters, plot, and settings. • Show students that themes can apply to different stories; themes grow out of stories. • Show how you make personal connections to a character, problem, conflict, or setting. • Ask the student to connect to a character's situation, personality, problems, or friendships. • Help the student use what he or she knows about a narrative element and use that prior knowledge to infer.
Inferring With Informational Texts	• Recalls facts but is unable to interpret the facts. • Can't connect the information to other situations.	• Make sure the student has background knowledge of the topic to bring to the inferring process. If not, build and enlarge student's prior knowledge.

(continued on next page)

Strategy	Student Behaviors	Scaffolding and Reteaching
(Inferring With Informational Texts, continued)	• Unable to connect to ways the information changed people's lives. • Unable to show how the information changed his or her thinking. • Can't explain what the facts mean. • Unable to explain why this information matters to self, others, community, or world issues and problems.	• Show how you use what you know about a topic to figure out what the facts mean. • Help students determine why the facts matter by asking why they matter to people, animals, or nature. Making the questions specific can support inferring. • Model how you use what you know to connect the information to yourself, peers, and others, and to ways people live, to oil supplies, to food supplies, to medicine, etc. • Ask questions such as, "How can information save lives or improve our quality of life?" • Work one-on-one until student shows he or she is ready to work with a peer or independently.
Determining Importance	• Cannot explain the strategy. • Avoids previewing. • Doesn't set purposes for reading. • Sees no purpose in skimming for details. • Doesn't know how to skim. • Doesn't bring what he or she knows to the preview or reading. • Has difficulty taking notes. • Resists taking notes. • Says the text is too difficult. • Has little to no prior knowledge of topic. • Doesn't know how to use a web to take notes. • Can't find big ideas. • Doesn't make personal connections.	• Explain the importance of the preview for background knowledge and setting purposes for reading. • Practice, with the student, previewing text features and then using these to set purposes. • Model the preview, then set purposes and have student do part of the work. Slowly, release the process to the student. • In a novel, the student previews the title, cover illustration, chapter titles, and reads the first page. • Model how having purposes from a preview helps read for, then select key details. • Observe student using the purposes he or she set to read and choose key details. Do this with short sections of text and add more text when the student shows readiness. • Work with individuals or pairs and always start the scaffold with your think-alouds, then have students practice with you. • Show student how to place key details on a sticky note while reading. • Show student how to skim for key details after reading and jot these on a web. • Show students how you bring what you know about a topic or narrative element to support choosing key details. • Encourage student to make personal connections to the text and use the connections to explain what's important. • Show student how you can find big ideas by asking what the key details mean and why they are important to our lives.
Synthesizing	• Retells instead of summarizing. • Has difficulty creating new understandings. • Doesn't bring what he or she knows to the text. • Doesn't understand that as you read, you are adjusting your opinions because you collect more information.	• Explain and practice aspects of synthesizing one at a time: summarizing, building new understandings, adjusting opinions while reading, and finding theme and main ideas. • Think-aloud to model each element of synthesizing. Then have student practice with you. • Gradually release the process to the student. • To summarize fiction/biography use Somebody Wanted But So. • To summarize informational texts, use Topic, 3 Key Facts, How Text Changed Thinking About Topic.

(*After Reading: Think With Details to Create New Understandings*, continued)

Strategy	Student Behaviors	Scaffolding and Reteaching
(Synthesizing, continued)	• Struggles to generalize main ideas and themes from details.	• Show student how asking questions about the author's purposes can help them find the theme. • Demonstrate how key details, along with the purpose for reading, can help readers find the main ideas. • Paired Discussions: Have pairs discuss what they know about the topic for a narrative element of the text so they can make personal connections that can lead them to exploring theme. • Model how you change your opinions about a character or conflict as you go from the beginning to the middle and the end of a text. Point out the events, interactions, and actions that caused the change. Explain that lived-through events change people and characters. • Show how you adjust your ideas about information as you learn more and as you bring what you know to the facts. • Model how the reading changes your notions of a topic, narrative element, or genre by going back to what you knew at the start of the reading to where you are now that you have finished.
Visualizing	• Unable to create mental pictures of words, narrative elements, or new information. • Does not use the five senses to create mental images. • Sees nothing while reading. • Does not know that seeing is like writing—it's a measure of comprehension and assists recall and memory.	• Show how you find words in the text that paint images. Next, explain that these words help you see a part of the text in your mind. • Tell students that making mental pictures while reading is like making your own movie, but the screen is your mind. • Explain that good readers make mental pictures because it keeps them interested and shows understanding. • Have the student choose words from a passage that make strong images, then describe the picture he or she imagines. • Model how words that relate to the five senses—see, hear, smell, taste, feel—can help readers make mental pictures. • Have the student find sensory words in a passage and use these to make mental pictures. • Model how making mental pictures—having visual memory—helps you recall details. • Ask the student to use his or her mental pictures to retell many details and explain what these mean.
Building Vocabulary	• Has limited vocabulary for the topic. • Lacks knowledge of the concepts in the text. • Doesn't connect prior knowledge to new words and concepts. • Little to no knowledge of prefixes, suffixes, and roots.	• Preteach important words. • Preteach concepts and related words. • Teach prefixes to show how these change the meaning of words. • Teach suffixes and show how these indicate parts of speech. • Teach roots and stems so students can use this knowledge to figure out the meaning of an unfamiliar word. • Model how knowing something about a similar word can help you figure out the meaning of a new, but related, word.

Continue to Reflect and Wonder . . .

Give yourself the gift of time when you are changing or adding teaching practices to your instructional repertoire. Start small with conferring. You'll know when you feel comfortable. That's the time to stretch yourself to do a bit more. Revisit the questions that follow; they will help you set a comfortable pace for change and accept that trying to do everything at once is counterproductive to the goal of implementing effective or different practices.

◆ What kinds of independent work choices and guidelines for getting help do I give students so I can confer without interruptions?

◆ How am I focusing my conferences before I meet with students?

◆ How can I make sure that my conferences don't go over five minutes?

◆ How can I structure the conference so the student does most of the talking, and I do most of the listening?

◆ Once I complete a conference, how do I use the data?

◆ How do the conferences and assessments I collect affect the scaffolds and instruction I plan?

CHAPTER 4

Assessing Tiered Learning Tasks

*I*t's mid-October. I'm conferring with Brian, an eighth grader reading on a fifth-grade level. "I'm doing good here," he tells me. "But I'm failing history, science, and English. What's the point?" Brian waves his hand around the classroom, implying that this class is a waste of time. "I'll never pass other stuff."

In classrooms throughout this country, similar scenes occur repeatedly. There's truth in Brian's feelings. He is part of a special reading class that meets daily; this class is in addition to his regular 45-minute English class. The school sincerely wanted to support Brian and students like him, who read instructionally three to five years below eighth-grade level. However, the self-confidence that resulted from experiencing success with reading, discussing, and writing about reading in the special class disappeared when these students entered other classes. In the special reading class, Brian and his classmates read books they chose on topics that interested them, and most important, books they could read and understand. Tiering in this setting meant that students used books below eighth-grade reading levels, but they applied eighth-grade skills and strategies to these texts. Brian, whose first book was *Babe Ruth* by Matt Christopher, discussed obstacles Babe faced, people and events that influenced his life, and the contributions he made to baseball and to people. Because Brian could gather details from this book, he had the information he needed to draw conclusions about Babe, discuss the influences in his life, and so on.

So why did Brian and others feel defeated, discouraged, and at times angry? Though tiering occurred in the special reading class by giving students books they could read, analyze, and think with, Brian and his classmates were assigned to "read" grade-level texts in other classes. Not only weren't those reading materials tiered, but teachers required students to complete the same writing assignments and take the same tests. I began to feel that providing success with reading in one class worked against these struggling readers because a daily lack of success in other classes outweighed learning experiences in the tiered reading class.

Moreover, Brian and his classmates needed far more practice with reading than skilled readers in order to improve and eventually become grade-level readers. Texts and tasks needed to be tiered in *all subjects*, with teachers asking students to think at high levels using materials students could read and understand. Instead, students like Brian receive help in one class and sit passively in other classes, unable to read the texts, contribute to discussions, complete written work, or pass quizzes and tests. Daily, this negative tide pulls below-grade-level readers backward in skill, vocabulary development, and attitude toward learning (Allington, 2001, 2002, 2006a, 2006b; Allington & Cunningham, 2002; Anderson, 1992). In this chapter, you'll see how tiering reading materials and required and choice assignments can reverse these negative trends while improving students' reading skills, vocabulary, and writing about reading in journals, paragraphs, and short essays. And as students experience success, self-confidence and motivation increases, enabling students to move forward (Guthrie and Wigfield, 2000; Guthrie, 2004).

As You Continue to Read . . .

First, I'll also discuss ways to tier assignments, projects, and other student work so every student works where he or she can succeed. This means that if a student reads a below-grade-level book or completes a paragraph instead of an essay, the student practices grade-level thinking and analytical skills, whether the task is required or a student's choice. You'll also see that choice, independent reading is a natural way to tier because students choose books that are easy to read and about topics that interest them. Then, you'll read and reflect on tiering a variety of tasks, including journal and essay writing, individual and group projects, paired and small-group discussions, and homework. You'll explore literacy vignettes that illustrate how checklists can help you assess what areas students need support in during instructional conferences. I'll also provide suggestions for grading tiered tasks and a chart that offers scaffolding and reteaching suggestions for tiering reading and other tasks. The chapter closes with suggestions for professional development and the reflective section, "Continue to Reflect and Wonder . . ."

Forms For Chapter 4 That You'll Find on the CD

Checklists for Required Tasks
- Analytical Essays and Paragraphs (Form 43)
- Analytical Writing (Form 44)
- Note-Making (Form 45)
- Graphic Organizers (Form 46)

Journal Entries:
- Drawing Conclusions About a Person or Character (Form 47)
- Connecting an Issue to a Text (Form 48)
- Making Inferences (Form 49)
- Visualizing (Form 50)
- Content and Conventions Feedback From Students' Journals (Form 51)

Checklists for Choice Tasks
- Oral and Written Book Reviews (Form 52)
- Diary Entries and Letters Characters Might Write and for Interviews With Characters (Form 53)
- Fine Arts Projects (Form 54)
- Writing Activities, Visuals, and Advertisements (Form 55)

Book Conference Forms
- Fiction (Form 56)
- Nonfiction (Form 57)
- Biography: Obstacles a Person Faced (Form 58)
- Relationships (Fiction or Biography) (Form 59)
- Drawing Conclusions About a Person's Personality (Form 60)
- Peer Book Conference (Form 61)

Tiering: More Work vs. the Complexity of Assignments

Tiering *does not mean* that we give proficient readers and writers longer assignments and more books to complete. Students view this strategy as punishment. Here's what a seventh grader wrote about having to complete a project on every independent reading book.

As soon as I saw that others who read the minimum requirements had much less work to do, I started entering in my book log the minimum number of books to be read for a [specific] month. Why do six projects when I could do two and then read what I wanted to read anyway? She [the teacher] wants a grade for everything. I know the game and I'm only reporting the minimum number [of completed books].

Students quickly figure out the rules that govern teacher's decisions.

However, tiering *does mean* adjusting assignments to the learning needs and abilities of individual students. Brain researcher David Sousa (2001) provides excellent tiering guidelines for us teachers. Sousa recommends that we first consider the difference between the "difficulty" and the "complexity" of an assignment. Instead of asking students to read and write more, thereby increasing the difficulty, teachers need to design activities that increase in complexity. So, a struggling reader might work on a written summary of a book for a book review and present the opinion part of her review orally, while proficient learners might write a book review that includes a brief summary and a supported opinion. As another example, a requirement might be that all students have to be able to show how and why a character changes from the beginning to the end of a story. Tiering this assignment might look like this: All learners will complete a graphic organizer. Students who struggle will collaborate with and receive support from the teacher to transform the notes into a paragraph, while proficient learners will complete the paragraph with feedback from a partner. Adjusting reading and writing tasks and oral presentations to meet the needs of each learner insures success followed by feelings of pleasure and satisfaction while learning. Tiering can mean adjusting:

- ◆ the reading level of a text so students use materials they can read at their instructional levels;
- ◆ the writing tasks a student does so that those who need support at the sentence and paragraph level receive it while others write longer pieces;
- ◆ the choice projects you offer so they meet the needs of the range of reading and writing levels in your classes;
- ◆ presentations of choice learning, such as an illustrated time line or a photo essay, that include the high-level thinking you expect at your grade level;
- ◆ the amount of independent, choice reading so that thick, hefty books count as two to three titles;
- ◆ the kinds of reading materials for struggling readers so that they read more, because texts are easy and on topics that interest them;
- ◆ the choice of assignments in paired and group projects so they meet the learning needs of diverse members;
- ◆ homework assignments so students are truly reading at their independent levels and completing writing tasks that match what they can do well; and
- ◆ tests and quizzes by having students respond to what you are teaching using instructional and/or independent reading materials.

Benefits of Tiering

Developing tasks that students can succeed at means that you are also building students' self-confidence, motivation, and the inner voice that says, *I can do this!* Brian and his classmates deepened my understanding of the need to match texts and tasks to students, because when these students experienced success with reading, writing, and analyzing texts in their special class, they became engaged learners who wanted to repeat these successes (Guthrie & Wigfield, 2000). What discouraged these students was returning to learning at their frustration levels in other subjects.

Tiering reading tasks and texts means that students read books and complete assignments that are within their learning reach; Vygotsky called this the zone of proximal development (1978). I call it the teaching and learning zone. In the teaching and learning zone, students can move forward with the support of their teacher and/or a peer expert. Here's what matching texts and tasks to students means. If a seventh grader reads instructionally at third grade, that seventh grader should apply grade-level skills and high-level reading strategies to the easier text. All students, no matter what their instructional reading levels, should engage in the high-level, analytical thinking expected for their grade using materials they *can* read. To improve as a reader and to enlarge reading vocabulary, students need to learn at their instructional levels, think at high levels, and complete a great deal of independent, practice reading (Anderson et al., 1988; Ambruster et al., 2001; Block & Mangieri, 2002; Block & Reed, 2003; Buehl, 2001; Gambrell, 2007; Guthrie et al., 1999; Krashen, 1993; Nagy & Anderson, 1984; Reutzel et al., 1991; Snow et al., 1998).

Because tiering invites teachers to adjust assignments and reading materials, you might see this as adding more to your workload. There will be times that you'll feel this is asking too much and your own frustration levels will escalate. My teaching experiences help me relate to these feelings. However, I'm hoping that you'll put these feelings aside as you explore suggestions for tiering both required and choice tasks because I have included the support you need to succeed.

Tiering Required Tasks

If your teaching position is like mine, then your school district requires that you teach certain genres in reading and specific kinds of writing such as persuasive and informative essays. Tiering reading texts when teaching a genre is easy as long as your school district does not insist that you use one text for all students. Here, you would choose texts within a genre, such as realistic fiction, that match students' instructional reading levels. (See pages 33–43 for suggestions on estimating students' instructional reading levels.)

Independent reading is a crucial required task, for it provides opportunities for students to practice and apply what they've learned during instructional reading.

Independent reading also builds vocabulary knowledge as students meet words in different contexts and enlarges readers background knowledge. By choosing books that are easy to read, books below their instructional levels, students naturally tier this all-important learning experience.

Tiering required writing tasks, however, can become a tough issue because you might feel that you are not fulfilling basic grade-level requirements. However, keep in mind that if a student can't write a cohesive paragraph, then that student will not be able to write the required essay. In fact, that student will be writing at his or her frustration level. Better to teach students to write a solid paragraph because then they have the building block of the essay (Robb, 2004). There will be times when tiering involves more scaffolding, which means that you might give extra support to a student at the planning stage so he or she can complete the writing assignment successfully.

For different types of writing about reading, I've provided suggestions for tiering on pages 81–85. Whatever adjustments you make for students, always ask them to use their reading to think at high levels and apply grade-level skills and strategies to their texts. In addition, I always find it helpful to ask students, *What kinds of adjustments do you need to be successful?* Here are some responses from students; note how they often point the way for tiering:

> For more details on organizing and implementing whole-class differentiated reading instruction, see my book *Differentiating Reading Instruction* (2008).

"I need more time—I work slow." —fourth grader

"I write more on the computer." —eighth grader

"I need to talk to you first, write after." —fifth grader

"Can I draw and write?" —seventh grader

"I need to write less." —fourth grader

"Can you help me get started?" —sixth grader

Tiering Choice Tasks

For every unit of study, I offer students choice projects. The list of these projects can be generated by you, by the students, or a combination of you and students. I prefer the list be a combination of ideas from me and students. Because the culture and needs of each class differs, the kinds of projects and activities will differ, especially if the list responds to students' needs and level of writing and reading skill. A list with projects that include oral and written work and the fine arts (see page 77) will meet the needs of diverse learners because tiering has been built into the choices. Remember, though, that *all students*, in oral or written presentations, will demonstrate their ability to connect choice projects to themes, issues, and strategies.

I find that most of the time students choose activities that they can do well. If you feel a student has chosen an activity that is too difficult, talk to the student. If the desire is strong, make sure that you provide the scaffolding needed for the student to succeed. If one of your best students chooses an easy project, that's okay as long as this does not occur throughout the year. No one wants to work at a demanding level all the time. Students need breaks as much as adults. Remember, too, that all projects will invite students to discuss an issue, explore a theme, analyze character, and so on. These connections occur when students present their projects. A discussion of an illustrated timeline of a book could also include points about text structure, themes, personal and text connections, or a discussion of how a character changed and the causes of these changes.

You can invite students to suggest projects and add a few of your own. Having about ten choices works well for me, but make sure that students know the structure of each choice so they can succeed. Some students will ask to complete projects not on the list; it's fine as long as the student has a knowledge of the genre. That's why negotiating the list with students is helpful, because they offer the genres they know. The list of twenty *choice assessments* that follows illustrates the wide range of activities that can be offered during a unit of study.

> Tiered assignments include adjustments for students who struggle, for ELL (English Language Learners) students, and for grade-level and proficient learners.

Possible Choice Activities

For each project, students will have to connect their work to the issue and themes we've discussed, to text structures, and to inferential thinking about characters or people, conflicts, problems, events, interactions, and so on.

- Illustrated timeline of four to six events
- Readers Theater script
- Cartoons that show problems/solutions
- Interview between two characters
- Newspaper story
- Letters between two characters
- Illustrations of two to three events
- Written book review
- Advice column responding to letter from a character or a person
- Interview between two people from the same or different biographies

- Dramatic monologue
- Illustrations of key settings or problems from a text
- Radio play
- Diary entries
- Letters to a character
- Oral book talk
- Poem about a character, theme, conflict
- Illustrations of four symbols in text
- Advertisement for a book
- Song lyrics about a character, person, theme, conflict, or event

Using Checklists to Assess Tiered Tasks

Assessing tiered tasks means that you are tiering required and choice reading and writing assignments. However, when you adjust assignments and the materials students read, you are tiering all classroom work in order to meet the learning needs of each student. The checklists in this section and on the CD contain a list of things to look for that enable you to monitor a range of learners, from those who struggle to proficient readers and writers. On each list, you'll attend to those items that link you to the diverse tiered assignments students have completed.

Read the checklists carefully and choose the list that enables you to evaluate the tiered tasks you are studying, which may include:

◆ reading skills and strategies;

◆ connections to themes and issues;

◆ journal writing about reading;

◆ knowledge of genre and text structures;

◆ behaviors while reading, writing, and listening; and

◆ presentations.

Complete checklists you've selected two to three times a year for grade-level and proficient readers. For those who struggle and for English Language Learners, complete checklists you've selected every four to six weeks—more if you feel this will benefit the student. Save paper by using one checklist for the entire year. Date each observation and use a different colored pen or pencil to record these. You can use students' journals, analytical paragraphs and essays, book reviews, and paired and group discussions, book talks, and presentations of projects, as well as your observational notes and conferences to complete checklists. You might decide to focus on one aspect of tiered work such as several journal entries, book talks, or projects.

If I don't have enough observational notes of tiered tasks to help me complete a checklist, I find it helpful to hold a brief conference and invite students to show me how they apply a strategy or to discuss their knowledge of text structure, issues, and themes. The items you review on the checklist should always relate to your teaching, what students do well, areas that need attention, and what you hope students will learn.

Using Checklists to Confer to Determine How to Tier Reading

During my getting-to-know-you conference with Jake (pseudonym), I learned that he found reading "too hard" in all of his subjects. "I'm slow," he told me, "and don't get lots of words." The first step I took toward tiering reading materials for Jake was to conduct an oral reading error analysis (pages 38–42) which indicated that he was a

Student's Name_____ Reading Text _Marshfield Dreams by Ralph Fletcher_

Checklist for Strategies Students Use During Reading

Key: R=Rarely S=Sometimes U=Usually NO=Not Observed

During-Reading Strategies	Indicators That Student Uses The Strategy	Date 10/30/06	Key and Comments
Adjust Reading Rate	Changes purposes for reading a text, such as rereading, reading for pleasure, or reading to collect information and construct meaning.	NO	
Predict/Support/ Confirm/Adjust	Uses text to support predictions and to confirm and adjust them.	S	
Question	Asks questions while reading. Knows that the text may not answer all questions.	NO	
Make Connections	Connects to text using personal experiences and background knowledge.	S	
Visualizes	Creates mental pictures from details, from figurative language, from strong verbs and specific nouns in the text.		Has difficulty due to making meaning with text.
Monitor Understanding	Constructs meaning and identifies parts of text that are not understood. Uses questioning, making connections and visualizing to construct meaning.		Reads through punctuation. Unaware that punctuation supports making meaning.
Self-Correct	Can correct without help parts of the text that don't make sense. Has strategies to say and figure out the meaning of difficult words.		Needs fix-up strats and practice using context clues to figure out tough words.
Reread	Rereads to boost recall, to revisit favorite parts, and to understand confusing parts.		
Close Read	Breaks confusing parts into small chunks to close read. Brings prior knowledge and new information and vocabulary to the close reading process.		

Wants to improve — wants to learn to be a better reader. Great attitude.

**Figure 4.1** This reading strategy checklist gives me insight into a sixth grader's reading behaviors; see Form 24 on the CD.

sixth grader reading at an instructional fourth-grade level. I chose to complete a checklist that provided me with insight into Jake's during-reading behaviors to try to determine whether instructional level was the only issue (see Figure 4.1, Form 24 on the CD). The oral reading error analysis gave me data to complete the checklist, which revealed that Jake read through punctuation, even at his independent reading level, and had no fix-up strategies. Jake's self-evaluation of his reading showed me how much he valued reading and wanted to improve. "I want to read better. I watch [classmates] read and see they like it." The checklist and Jake's self-evaluation helped me develop an intervention plan for Jake. Because Jake valued reading and wanted to improve, an aspect of tiering not only included the level of instructional materials but also scaffolding conferences where I modeled self-monitoring and self-correcting, and Jake practiced these strategies.

Scaffolding conferences were five to seven minutes. I zoomed in on one issue, such as using punctuation to improve comprehension. I modeled, and Jake practiced with me and on his own. I also informed Jake's teachers of his determination to improve and asked them to find texts for him to read and learn from at his instructional reading level.

Intervention Plan for Jake

I've included this intervention plan so you can see that in conjunction with tiering, it's often necessary that we scaffold and/or reteach. Tiering, by offering Jake texts at his instructional level, was the first step I took. Next steps included scaffolding and reteaching conferences that would provide Jake with the fix-up strategies needed to succeed where he was.

Jake and I worked twice a week for three months. My goal was to teach Jake to self-monitor and give him Reread and Close Read as two fix-up strategies. During those months, I modeled and students practiced using context clues to figure out tough words; I also modeled Questioning the Author (Beck & McKeown, 2006). These strategies helped students improve vocabulary and unpack meaning from challenging texts. Here is what Jake and I worked on during short conferences:

- discuss punctuation and how it supports reading in meaningful chunks;
- model how to read using punctuation as a meaning-making guide;
- have Jake practice reading using punctuation to pause to check comprehension and recall. Ask Jake to discuss how this helps;
- introduce, model, and have Jake practice a self-monitoring strategy using a check for "understand it" and a question mark for "confused";
- introduce, model, and have Jake practice the fix-up strategy Reread; and
- introduce, model, and have Jake practice the fix-up strategy Close Read.

Using Checklists to Confer: Tiering to Improve Independent Reading

It's the second week of school, and students and I are still working on establishing routines and preparing for our first differentiated unit on suspense. Sixth-grader Adam still exhibits difficulty settling down during independent reading time. He changes books two to three times in twenty-five minutes. He paces. He goes to the bathroom. He makes clicking sounds while browsing. On three consecutive days, I make detailed notes on the checklist that monitors independent reading (Figure 4.2). Usually, I don't complete an independent reading checklist so early in the school year. However, Adam's behaviors tell me that I need to meet with him to discover how I can support him. During our first meeting, I share the checklist with Adam and ask, *Why are you having difficulty finding a book and reading?* It takes two more conferences and repeating the same question before Adam answers. "I don't like any [books]," he explains, pointing to the bookshelves. "If I don't like 'em, I don't read."

On his Interest Inventory, Adam writes that he likes comics and magazines about fishing. "Bring some comics and magazines into class," I suggest. "I'll bring some in, too."

"You mean it?" he asks, a puzzled look on his face.

"You bet," I reply.

The next day, Adam brings three comic books to school. Because of his high energy level, Adam reads his comic while standing at a counter. My job is to take Adam where he is with independent reading and provide him with materials he cares about—materials he'll read. The next week, I decide to book talk and display several graphic novels that are in my class library. There'll be no pressure on Adam to read one of these. I'm hoping that his curiosity will draw him to looking through these books and checking one out. Adam does check out an R.L. Stine graphic novel but warns me, "This doesn't mean I'll read it." But he does. "Not bad," he comments. "Any more like this?"

Using Checklists to Confer: Tiering to Improve Paragraphs and Essays About Reading

If I gave the class a choice of two to three thesis statements about a character, conflict, event, or theme, sixth grader Maria was able to find details to support the thesis. However, developing a thesis on her own and framing an introduction that ended in a thesis statement was a task Maria struggled with. On her own, Maria began an analytical paragraph about Louis Braille with, "I'm going to tell what I

Checklist for Monitoring Independent Reading

Student's Name _Adam_   Date _Sept._

OBSERVATIONS	TEACHER'S NOTES	DATES OBSERVED
Book Log Entries ◆ Number of books ◆ Variety of titles	No books listed from summer or by the end of the second week of reading time each day	9/7, 9/8, 9/12, 9/14
Independent Reading ◆ Selects books on comfort or recreational level. ◆ Gets started quickly. ◆ Self-helps before seeking peer or teacher assistance. ◆ Shows pleasure in reading through talk, projects, journal entries. ◆ Concentrates on book. ◆ Changes books several times during a silent reading period. ◆ Frequently talks to others. ◆ Occasionally stops and shares a favorite part.	Shows difficulty selecting books Avoids reading Appears to not be able to concentrate yes Sometimes Not happening at this point.	

ADDITIONAL NOTES AND COMMENTS:

Set up a meeting with Adam to discover reasons for Adam's avoidance of independent reading.

Figure 4.2 *My observations on this checklist spur me to hold a conference early in the year with sixth grader Adam, so I can discover how to support him; see Form 25 on the CD*

learned about Louis Braille." Then she proceeded to retell parts of the book: *Louis Braille: The Boy Who Invented Books for the Blind* by Margaret Davidson (1971). I had developed a short checklist for some students to evaluate their planning stage; the checklist came from the more detailed checklist on page 85. Maria's plan informed me that she needed some scaffolding for developing a thesis statement. Tiering for Maria meant she would not have to write a developed introduction that included her thesis statement. At this point, the thesis statement would be Maria's introduction. Once Maria had a thesis, I knew that she could find support because she was able to do this with a thesis statement I had created. You can see an example of the list of scaffolds the checklist helped me develop for Maria below. It's important to note that while I worked one-on-one with Maria, I was creating thesis statements and listing supporting details with the entire class using my read-aloud biography, *Sojourner Truth: Ain't I a Woman?* by Patricia and Frederick McKissack.

Scaffolds for Maria

Though I tiered the writing of the introduction for Maria, I wanted to help her integrate a thesis into an elaborated introduction. *This is what tiering is all about*—creating tasks students can accomplish. Once they experience success and can work independently, it's time to add another layer—in this case an introduction that includes a thesis.

Maria and I conferred for five minutes a day for five consecutive days. I chose to delay helping Maria integrate her thesis into an introduction until she practiced writing her own thesis. For now, the thesis statement served as her topic sentence. Here is what I planned for the series of conferences:

- ◆ explain that a thesis takes a position; the position can be positive or negative;

- ◆ model, using a read-aloud text, how I think through developing a thesis. Have Maria create a thesis based on the read-aloud;

- ◆ review what a thesis statement is. Model again; have Maria create a thesis statement; and

- ◆ help Maria discuss different positions or opinions she could develop based on Louis Braille's life. Create two thesis statements based on Braille's life.

Here are the two thesis statements Maria developed. For her plan, she will choose whether she wants to defend the positive or negative thesis. Being able to frame both perspectives offers students choice, as long as each statement can be supported with the text.

1. Braille was (was not) determined to develop an alphabet for blind people so they could read.

2. Braille had to fight hard (not fight hard) to get his system of writing and reading accepted by those who could see.

Mini-Checklist Developed for Maria and Five Other Students

Actually, to save time, I circled areas I would focus on using the long checklist (page 85). However, I've created a mini-checklist below so you can see what I evaluated on students' plans. The checklist, along with my observations and reading of students' plans, helped me decide who would benefit from scaffolding and who could use their plans to write a first draft of an analytical paragraph.

	WRITING CRITERIA	NOTES	DATES OBSERVED
Introduction/ Lead	• Can create a thesis statement that shows an opinion and/or position. • States thesis positively and negatively. • Chooses the position he or she wants to support.		
Supporting Details on Plan	• Has three pieces of support from the text. • Support includes specific details that the writer can elaborate. • Support includes vocabulary appropriate for topic.		

Name _____ Type of Writing _____

Analytical Writing Assessment Checklist

The checklist attends to the basic parts of the paragraph and essay—the lead or introduction, the body, and the conclusion—as well as voice, style, and writing conventions. Use the checklist for students to self-evaluate their piece as well as for peer and teacher evaluation. You can use all or parts of the checklist; you can focus on the writing criteria or standards you and your students established. Most important, tier the checklist by adapting it to your students' needs, including items that reflect your teaching and students' development. You'll find versions of the checklist on the CD; see Forms 43 and 44.

Name _____ Type of Writing _____

Checklist to Assess Analytical Writing

	WRITING CRITERIA	NOTES	DATES OBSERVED
Introduction/ Lead	• Catches reader's attention. • Includes a thesis. • Creates a developed introduction. • Transitions to next paragraph.		
Body	• Each paragraph starts with a clear introductory sentence. • Includes specific details from the text. • Develops ideas with sentences that include: *descriptions, definitions, examples, elaboration, cause/effect, compare/contrast.* • Thoroughly develops one idea in each paragraph. • Arranges ideas in a logical order. • Makes a logical argument. • Transitions to the next paragraph.		
Conclusion	• Restates thesis and moves beyond the thesis by: *making a judgment, endorsing an issue, discussing facts implied in the essay.*		
Writer's Voice	• Speaks in a convincing manner. • Shows interest in/feels strongly about the topic. • Uses positive language. • Writes in the active voice.		
Word Choice	• Explains important words/concepts. • Avoids clichés. • Language reveals an understanding of the topic. • Uses unique figurative language. • Includes strong verbs and specific nouns.		
Sentence Style	• Varies sentence openings. • Varies sentence length. • Sentences flow smoothly into one another. • Includes quotes.		
Writing Conventions (*List those you have included in your criteria.*)	• Writes with complete sentences. • Writes in paragraphs. • Uses correct spelling. • Uses commas correctly. • Has subject–verb agreement. • Uses direct quotations correctly. • Understands singular and plural possessives.		

Assessment Checklists and Grading Tiered Work

Checklists can show you what to look for when reviewing tiered assignments, and what you look for will differ for each student. Checklists can also help you formulate a grade for students' work. I give students the grade they've earned whether the task is more advanced or adjusted for an ELL student or struggling learner. Otherwise, students functioning below grade level will always receive low grades, which discourages working hard to improve.

Teachers worry about giving a struggling learner an A or a B because they feel it sends the message to parents and to next year's teachers that this is a proficient learner. It's unfair, however, to give ELL students and struggling learners low grades; it destroys motivation and the development of self-confidence and self-esteem. What I do is inform parents and note on the student's permanent record and/or report card that this child earned an A completing grade-level skills, strategies, and writing about reading using reading materials three years below grade level. I also point out whether the student can apply grade-level reading skills and strategies to materials at his or her instructional reading level.

Grading Guidelines When Differentiating Reading Instruction

Before I tackle grading at school, it's helpful to understand the various layers or zones of assessment that impact grading and affect students' self-confidence and feelings of efficacy. Schools grade students when they take mandated tests; schools also grade teachers and base these grades on students' performance on state tests and administrative evaluations. However, grading is more than the work students complete at school. The concentric circles in Figure 4.3 illustrate the zones or layers of assessment. Peers, parents, home values, and siblings also influence students' performance and achievement at school. These multiple zones affect the learning attitudes and performance of students, and their level of investment in and commitment to learning at home and school, as well as their achievement and grades.

At workshops I facilitate on differentiation, several teachers always ask three questions: "But how do you grade students' work?" "What work do you grade?" and "Do you collect enough assessments to form a grade?" These are important questions to consider and discuss because the reality is that we have to put grades on report cards. In this section, I'm not going to suggest how to weight grades from tests, class work, writing, homework, and projects because school districts have their own guidelines that teachers must follow. Grading is one of those never-ending topics that teachers discuss annually at faculty meetings. I will discuss five areas of grading, hoping that my thoughts will ignite many conversations about this topic:

◆ the purposes;

◆ the problems;

◆ what can be graded;

◆ setting criteria for grading; and

◆ combining tradition and common sense.

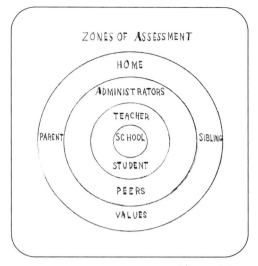

Figure 4.3

These zones guide my thinking about assessment and grading

The Purposes of Grading

Grading seems to be a tradition in American schools. Below, I've listed some purposes of grading, purposes we accept often without questioning them:

◆ to measure achievement;

◆ to evaluate students' progress;

◆ to determine whether students will be promoted or will graduate;

◆ to figure out students' class and school standings;

◆ to complete report cards and satisfy tradition; and

◆ to meet district requirements.

The reason grading is on the never-ending annual discussion list is because establishing and using grades poses many problems for teachers and students.

The Problems Grading Poses

It's beneficial to confront and discuss the problems you see and experience with grading. The list that follows outlines some drawbacks grading poses:

◆ It's often subjective, especially if the teacher does not use a rubric or set of grading criteria that have been negotiated with students.

◆ It provides a limited picture of a child's achievement by spotlighting tests and finished products over process and daily work.

◆ It encourages teaching to the tests, whether the tests are mandated by the state or a common assessment for history, science, math, and English that a school has developed.

◆ It's based on the assumption that students should be measured the same way using the same materials and tasks.

◆ It discourages viewing the child as unique with strengths and needs that differ from classmates.

◆ It can promote the belief that learning and achievement are equal to testing well.

In an educational system where grades are a tradition, trying to not grade also poses specific problems. Several years ago, I wrote a letter to parents explaining why I preferred writing narratives about students' progress rather than giving a letter or number grade. Not only did parents and students object, but the school objected; grades were needed to determine graduation prizes, class and school standing, and placement in high school classes. Grading is here to stay. Teachers can grade anything from the quality of students' responses in a discussion to all written work, including tests, quizzes, and homework.

What Teachers Can Grade

For me, it's important to not grade everything that students do that relates to school. Why? Because I want students to take risks and learn from mistakes without worrying about grades. I also feel that all the work students do at school should not be motivated by a grade, but by the desire to learn and share ideas. Remember, every writing, homework, and class assignment does not have to be graded. What to grade is a decision you can make with input from your students. When grading writing, I encourage you to view students' process and progress from brainstorming, to planning, to drafting, to revising, and then final draft. The list below includes suggestions of what you might grade:

- ◆ tests and quizzes;
- ◆ written work: paragraphs, essays, some journal work, book reviews— including brainstorming, planning sheets, drafts, and so on;
- ◆ homework;
- ◆ projects; and
- ◆ class work.

Set Criteria to Make Grading More Objective

It is helpful to set criteria or guidelines with students before they begin a project or task. Criteria let students know what you will be grading and provides them with guidelines for self- and peer evaluation. The criteria you and students establish should relate to what you've taught and modeled and what students have practiced. Criteria also enable you to explain why a student achieved a certain grade. For example, here are the criteria students and I establish for a journal entry that asks them to infer the protagonist's personality traits and offer support from the text:

Criteria for "Personality Traits and Prove It"

- ◆ Heading includes student's name, date, title, and author of book.
- ◆ Use double entry format. On the left side write the protagonist's name.
- ◆ List, on the left side, four personality traits. Leave five to six lines between each trait.
- ◆ Note for each trait, on the right side, specific details that enabled you to infer this trait.
- ◆ Write details in your own words.

◆ Look back in your book and reread parts, before writing the details, to ensure that you are as specific and detailed as possible.

You can print the criteria you and your students establish on chart paper as a resource for the class or you can give each student a copy. Students receive this before they complete the assignment so they know their responsibilities and what you will comment on and grade. Having the criteria provides you with specific points to comment on to show what students did well and point out areas that need improvement. Remember, since criteria grow out of your teaching and what students have shown you they can do, it's easy to establish guidelines for each task. You can tier criteria for students who need accommodations. To tier the journal criteria, for example, I have some students find one or two personality traits and offer support. Or I gradually release responsibility to the student by modeling the task with one trait, working with the student on a second trait, and asking her to complete a third independently.

Professional Books on Differentiation and Tiering

- *The Differentiated Classroom: Responding to the Needs of All* by Carol Ann Tomlinson, ASCD, 1999.

- *Differentiation: From Planning to Practices, Grades 6–12* by Rick Wormeli, Stenhouse, 2007.

- *Differentiating Reading Instruction: How to Teach Reading to Meet the Needs of Each Student* by Laura Robb, Scholastic, 2008.

- *Fair Isn't Always Equal: Assessing & Grading in the Differentiated Classroom* by Rick Wormeli, Stenhouse, 2006.

- *How to Differentiate Instruction in Mixed-Ability Classrooms* by Carol Ann Tomlinson, 2nd edition, ASCD, 2004.

- *Understanding by Design: Professional Development Workbook* by Jay McTighe, ASCD, 2004.

Scaffolding and Reteaching Chart for Tiered Tasks

Bringing a measure of common sense to teaching and grading does not have to interfere with the grading requirements of your school district. Have students complete the number of graded tasks and projects required by your school. In addition, however, include performance-based assessments and student self-evaluation because these inform your daily teaching decisions and support differentiating reading instruction. The chart on pages 90–91 will provide you with scaffolding and reteaching suggestions based on the writing and projects you've tiered to meet the needs of the diverse readers and writers in your classes.

Professional Development Suggestions

To deepen your knowledge of tiering in the differentiated classroom, I recommend that you form a group of interested colleagues to read and discuss one or all of the professional books listed in the box shown above. In addition, you'll want to meet regularly to discuss and share your experiences with tiering projects, writing, etc. This

Scaffolding and Reteaching Chart for Tiered Tasks

Task	Student Behaviors	Scaffolding and Reteaching Ideas
Journal Writing	• Writes little. • Retells, instead of selecting details. • Organizes pages incorrectly. • Avoids doing the writing.	• Tier and have students do less. • Have student draw responses and tell you about the drawings. • Schedule several short conferences and work one-on-one. • Release responsibility for part of the work, then all, when student shows you readiness.
Linking Issues to Texts	• Unable to explain issues in instructional and independent book. • Does not link issues to the read-aloud.	• Make sure the student understands the issue and what it means and implies. • Help the student connect the issue to his or her life or to current events. • Have student work with a peer. • Meet one-one-one to discuss the issue. • Meet again to model how to find the issue in the read-aloud first, then the student's text. • Confer with student until he or she is ready to complete this independently.
Finding Themes and Big Ideas	• Has difficulty finding theme in fiction, biography, or drama. • Doesn't preview and set purposes to find key details. • Has difficulty using important details or ideas to pinpoint key details and ideas.	• Think aloud using the read-aloud text to show how you find themes. • Help student see that theme can be tied to the author's purposes. • Stress the benefits of setting purposes before reading, then using the purposes to pinpoint key details and ideas. • Think aloud to show student how you use purposes and key details to figure out the big or main ideas. • Meet one-on-one to model finding themes or big ideas. Discuss your process. • Have the student practice the process and think aloud to show you his or her reasoning. Return to modeling if necessary. • Continue practicing until you feel the student is ready for gradual release. • Have student work with a peer for support on finding theme or big ideas.
Projects: Individual	• Turns in incomplete work. • Turns in work late. • Work is poorly done. • Appears uninterested. • Avoids completing during reserved class times.	• Meet with student and ask, "Why are you having difficulty with the project?" • Make sure that the choices offered include a range of projects that meet the learning needs of all students. • Offer to provide support. • Observe the student at work to determine if the project is too difficult.
Projects: Collaborative	• Doesn't contribute to group's effort. • Has no notes in journal. • Appears disinterested.	• Avoid this pattern by helping groups divide the workload among members. • Make sure the group, with your guidance, creates jobs that appeal to members and that the members can successfully complete.

Scaffolding and Reteaching Chart for Tiered Tasks, continued

Task	Student Behaviors	Scaffolding and Reteaching Ideas
Projects: Collaborative (_continued_)	• Doesn't participate in group's presentation.	• Decide whether student should work on a paragraph or an essay. • Confer at the planning stage. Help the student collect details and craft a topic sentence. • Confer to discuss the conclusion and what to include in it. • Discuss each detail and help student elaborate his or her ideas by asking questions. Jot down what the student says. Explain that asking questions and taking notes can lead to elaborating ideas. • Collaborate with a small group or the class and model the entire process.
Paragraphs and Essays	• Has difficulty writing a topic sentence. • Has difficulty writing an introduction or lead. • Avoids planning his or her writing. • Writes a few sentences. • Includes few specific details. • Doesn't elaborate details. • Doesn't write a conclusion.	• Tier homework assignments so each student can experience success completing independent work. • Make sure students can read homework material. • Vary writing tasks so each student experiences success.

ongoing give-and-take will support all group members and provide you with ideas that worked with colleagues' students and might work with yours.

Continue to Reflect and Wonder . . .

Tiering reading materials and learning tasks is an integral aspect of differentiating reading instruction. Our job is to reach and teach every learner, which means that not everyone can successfully complete the same assignment or read the same text. So, as you begin to tier reading materials, learning experiences, and tasks, revisit the questions that follow and keep in the forefront of your mind the fact that the children you and I teach can progress and improve as long as they can do the work.

◆ Why is it important to match texts to students' instructional reading levels?

◆ How do I involve students in tiering tasks?

◆ Why is it important to ask students to help me develop criteria for projects and writing?

◆ How do I know that students who read below grade level are thinking at or above grade level?

◆ How do I know when students require scaffolding and reteaching in order to complete a task successfully?

CHAPTER 5

Assess By Testing What You Teach

"Can't read Animal Farm, *so I can't pass tests."* —ninth grader

"Can't read lots of the words. Don't do the work." —seventh grader

"I'm dropping out next year." —tenth grader

Yes, these students have given up. Not only can't they cope with class work because class reading materials are at their frustration levels, but they don't pass school tests, exams, or state tests. Unfortunately, these students' futures are determined by state tests, one-size-fits-all reading materials, and common assessments where middle and high school students all take the same midterm and final exams—testing used to judge and punish instead of to support and improve. Without strong literacy skills, these students will struggle finding jobs and earning a living in a technological world where reading and writing well matter.

Tiering reading materials, tasks, and tests can break this cycle of failure because students work in their learning zone (Vygotsky, 1978) and work on writing assignments and projects that they can successfully complete. The question teachers ask is, *How can you test students who read different texts and are at diverse writing levels?* This chapter will explore answers to that question.

As You Continue to Read . . .

First, you'll compare traditional tests and quizzes to the kinds of tests you'll design when differentiating reading instruction. You'll explore suggestions for tiering tests to meet each child's strengths. Next, I'll discuss how often you should test students, as well as using tests to gain insights into students' study habits and process. You'll read about four sets of testing guidelines:

- for reading strategy tests;
- for vocabulary tests;
- for tests that grow out of journal prompts; and
- for essay tests.

You'll study models of different tests, consider the benefits of this type of testing, and explore suggestions for grading tests. The chapter closes with a short scaffolding and reteaching chart, suggestions for professional development, and "Continue to Reflect and Wonder . . ."

Testing What You Teach in the Differentiated Reading Classroom

In my classes and classes where I coach, the purpose of reading tests is to see if students can apply, on their own, what I've modeled and they've practiced independently.

Reading tests can focus on vocabulary and concepts; applying reading strategies; connecting issues, compelling questions, and themes to texts; figuring out why characters change; exploring what motivates characters' decisions and interactions, and so on. Tests can also assess students' knowledge of fiction and nonfiction text structures and how students complete journal prompts independently.

Because the differentiated reading teacher invites students to use diverse texts to think about issues such as human rights and explore compelling questions like *Is separate but equal just?*, students move beyond the facts (Gardner, 1999; Robb, 2008a; Sternberg, 2008). Therefore, assessments in these classrooms encourage thinking, analyzing, comparing and connecting ideas, and building new understandings, all with the goal of

---

Forms for Chapter 5 That You'll Find on the CD

Study Forms
- Study Skills Checklist (Form 62)
- Studying and Reviewing for a Social Studies or Science Test (Form 63)
- Reflections on My Test Performance (Form 64)
- Elements of Fiction (Form 65)
- Elements of Nonfiction (Form 66)

Tests
- Reading Strategy Test (Form 67)*
- Vocabulary Test: Word Map (Form 68)*
- Vocabulary Test: Concept Map (Form 69)*
- Vocabulary Test: Venn Diagram (Form 70)*
- Narrative Elements (Form 71)*
- Nonfiction Features (Form 72)*
- Journal Prompt Test: Making Inferences With Fiction (Form 73)
- Journal Prompt Test: Drawing Conclusions About a Character (Form 74)
- Journal Prompt Test: Making Inferences With Nonfiction (Form 75)

The forms are customizable on the CD.

> ## Tests and Other Assessments
>
> Tests ask students to complete a task in class in a specific amount of time. Students have more time to complete other assessments, such as essays and journal responses, and are able to follow a process that leads to success. Most teachers I work with feel they need to test all students using one set of questions, one kind of environment, and a specific time limit to establish a grade. It's possible to take this traditional notion of testing and tier tests so students answer the same open-ended questions or apply the same reading strategy, but use their instructional texts to respond. For me, the primary use of a test is to evaluate what students did well and identify areas where they still need scaffolding or reteaching. That's why I test what I'm teaching and students have been practicing once I feel that most can experience success. (See page 100 for a discussion of how often to test.)

developing responsible, creative, and thoughtful citizens. Though in a traditional class students might be tested on similar topics, the purpose, level of thinking, and materials differ when tiering tests.

Traditional and Tiered Tests

The chart that follows compares traditional and tiered tests. Note that the purpose of testing differs, as do the kinds of questions teachers ask. In addition, tiered tests in the differentiated reading classroom focus on thinking and analyzing at high levels.

Traditional Tests

◆ Purpose: assign a grade; move on to next topic.

◆ Questions test facts and memory.

◆ Tests for all are from the same texts, even if students can't read the text.

◆ Same test for all students.

◆ Poor performance is often not addressed.

◆ Mostly multiple choice, short answer, and/or matching questions.

◆ Teacher files completed test or the student takes it home, then tosses it.

Tiered Tests

◆ Purpose: to assess understanding; inform next instructional moves.

◆ Questions test application of facts to themes, issues, and compelling questions.

◆ Tests use students' instructional and/or independent reading texts.

◆ Tests can vary to meet students' strengths.

◆ Poor performance results in scaffolding and reteaching, not punishment.

◆ Mixture of short-answer questions and essays that require organization, thinking, and the application of strategies and information to big ideas.

◆ Both student and teacher mull over the test to identify strengths and needs, and to set goals for the next assessment.

Tiered Tests Inform Instructional Decisions

The test is as much for me as it is for the student. Before I move on, I have to make sure that *all students* have absorbed what's being tested. If not, then I need to make instructional decisions about who can work independently or move on to practicing other strategies and skills, who requires scaffolding, and which students would benefit from reteaching.

Ways to Tier Testing Materials

You have many choices, and what you do will vary and often depends on your ability to juggle multiple texts. Testing materials should be at students' instructional or independent reading levels, depending on your purpose for the assessment. You might test strategy application with instructional texts and application of an issue with an independent reading text. This is your call.

I always tell students what materials they'll use for the tests, encourage them to read the text several times, and have them use the materials during the test. Since tests move beyond memorizing facts, students can use materials to quote a passage, use context clues to figure out tough words. They can also quickly skim to find the support they'll use, for example, to show why a character changed or how their text illustrated justice and injustice. Here are some suggestions to consider:

1. You can use the same text for all students, but every student in your class should be able to read the text—it should be at the independent or instructional reading level of your weakest student.

2. You can choose two or three texts at different reading levels to meet your students' diverse needs.

3. You can use several chapters from students' instructional reading books.

4. You can ask students to use an independent reading book they've recently completed.

Your choices will vary year to year and depend on your comfort level and the diversity of reading levels in a specific class. I suggest collecting and filing short texts from magazines (see Appendix B, page 138, for a list) or from old, leveled basal readers and anthologies. The richer your collection, the easier it will be to find texts to meet students' reading levels. Share short texts that work for you with colleagues and invite them to share what they've collected so all of you can enlarge your collections.

Grading Tests

How you weight questions on your tests is your decision. I urge you to do this before handing students a test and note, on the test, the points questions are worth in parentheses after each question. Having this information enables students to budget their time and move on to weighty questions instead of sticking with a three- or five-point question they're struggling to answer.

Related to the grading process is teaching students how to read a test. Stress reading the entire test before plunging in and responding. Focus students' attention on directions and the point value of each question. Help them understand the benefits of budgeting time by suggesting time limits during the first marking period, then releasing responsibility for this to students. Keep supporting students who show you through class work and test results that they need you to help them process directions. In addition, point out how important reading, understanding, and following directions is to being successful. Make sure that you write your directions clearly and simply enough so your weakest reader can read and understand them.

Students' Feedback

I like to gather student feedback after some tests, especially if several have done poorly. The student samples and reproducible on pages 97–98 illustrate the value of inviting students to reflect on their preparation and test results.

However, be careful not to overuse the self-evaluation form. Be judicious and have students complete the form for a test you consider important. The form asks students to think about their performance and evaluate it. Unless students have to correct a test, they rarely look at it from the perspective of: *What did I answer well? What areas need strengthening? What can I do to improve my performance?* The more likely scenario is that the student looks at the grade and files or tosses the paper.

In addition, if students fail or do poorly, it's helpful to find out why this occurred from their perspective before the cycle of failure takes hold. You might discover that students don't know how to study and prepare for a test; that the text was too challenging; or that working independently posed problems that didn't arise when meeting with you or partnering with a peer.

When you ask students to complete the form, tell them that this will not be graded. You want honest answers that provide you with information you can use to plan interventions and scaffolds. If you schedule a conference with a student, build trust by pointing out positives and asking students how you can support them.

I've included the self-evaluations of a sixth-grade girl, Kayla (Figure 5.1), and Jonathan, a seventh-grade boy (Figure 5.2). Both names are pseudonyms. The part of Kayla's test on defining narrative elements and giving examples from a text was fine. She had difficulty showing why the protagonist changed from the beginning to the end of the short story. Kayla wrote:

"I can figure out the changes in personality. I can't find reasons for these.
I don't know how to do it."

Kayla's honesty helped me focus follow-up conferences on finding events, other characters, interactions, and decisions that cause changes. We practiced using the read-aloud text, then moved to Kayla's instructional book, *Shiloh* by Phyllis Reynolds

Name Kayla   **Date** Oct. 20

Reflections on My Test Performance

Directions: Answer the following questions. Be as specific as you can.

1. How did you prepare for this test?

   I read the story 3x.

2. How much time did you spend studying?

   Besides reading abt. 1 hr.

3. Can you explain why you think you earned a poor or excellent grade.

   Defining—I did great. I can figure out the changes in personalty. I cant find reasons for these. I dont know how to do it.

4. Was the reading material you used easy to understand? Explain.

   I could read it.

5. How can I support you?

   Help me find reason.

6. What can you do to insure that you improve and do better on the next test?

   Um — you help me.

Name Jon   **Date** Nov 6

Reflections on My Test Performance

Directions: Answer the following questions. Be as specific as you can.

1. How did you prepare for this test?

   I used the three days before the test to think about connections to- Was justice done? Explain. We could have notes, so I chose support before the test.

2. How much time did you spend studying?

   About 2 hours

3. Can you explain why you think you earned a poor or excellent grade.

   I did the thinking at home

4. Was the reading material you used easy to understand? Explain.

   Easy

5. How can I support you?

   I'm fine.

6. What can you do to insure that you improve and do better on the next test?

Naylor, and finally Kayla practiced on her own with a folk tale at her independent reading level.

Jonathan was an excellent reader who had a strong knowledge of strategies and the ability to infer and synthesize with fiction and nonfiction. In Figure 5.2, Jonathan's answer to the first question, "How did you prepare for this test?" illustrates that preparation over time results in having notes and ideas with support prior to taking the test. He wrote, "I used the three days before the test to think about connections: 'Was justice done? Explain.' We could have notes, so I chose my support before the test."

The purpose of this test was to observe how students used an independent reading

Name _____ Date _____

Reflections on My Test Performance

Directions: Answer the following questions. Be as specific as you can.

1. How did you prepare for this test?

2. How much time did you spend studying?

3. Explain why you think you earned your grade.

4. Was the reading material you used easy to understand? Explain.

5. How can I support you?

6. What can you do to ensure that you improve and do better on the next test?

book to connect to big ideas. For the test, students chose a recently completed biography or fictional book, then selected one of three compelling questions/prompts that related to their book. Questions and prompts have to be open-ended, not story-specific, so they can relate to any biography or fictional texts students read. Here are the three that I gave seventh graders:

◆ Was justice done? Explain.

◆ Discuss two injustices and explain the causes of each.

◆ How do people/characters cope with injustice? Choose a person or protagonist, present two injustices and discuss how the person/protagonist dealt with each one.

Note that the tiering was using a different independent reading book that each student chose. The expectation was that all students had to analyze their book using challenging questions/prompts. Avoid diminishing the thinking (Armstrong, 2008). Always have students use materials they can read and comprehend so they can analyze issues, themes, or compelling questions by connecting these to their text.

Jonathan selected Avi's *Nothing but the Truth: A Documentary Novel*. As he points out, because he thought about his answer before the test and arrived in class with detailed notes, he was able to write a thoughtful essay with solid examples from the book.

Students who waited to do all of the thinking in class did not have enough time to gather ideas and support, then write. My observations, along with students' self-evaluations, enabled me to separate those who had difficulty due to a lack of preparation from those who were unable to link their text to the questions. To improve organizational and study skills, I met with groups of three, discussed their self-evaluations, asked students how they could improve on the next test, and asked them to jot their goals on the back of their self-evaluations. When I announced the next test, I met with small groups, had students review their goals, then provided class time over three consecutive days for them to prepare. Giving up class time to teach study skills is worthwhile, for if students experience the benefits of advance preparation and do well, they are more likely to set aside time at home.

Those students who required extra practice connecting a question to their text worked with me individually or in pairs. Again, we practiced using a read-aloud text, then moved to students' texts. You can retest students you supported to see whether they can make these connections independently.

How Often Should I Test Students?

Teachers frequently ask me this question. I'm not a huge fan of frequent tests and quizzes in language arts. I have solid reasons for this decision, as students complete many in-class assessments: journal entries on issues, text structures, and applying a reading strategy; analytical paragraphs and essays; reading logs; book talks; and written book reviews. I also complete checklists, conference forms, and take observational notes.

It's reasonable to test students three to four weeks into a unit to determine what they've absorbed and pinpoint areas that need reinforcement. In addition, I test about seven to ten days before a unit ends so I still have time to scaffold the learning for those who need it. You can support students' needs by using reproducibles in my *Teaching Reading: A Differentiated Approach* (2008b). You'll find high-level thinking practice sheets for students who need scaffolding, for those who can work independently, and for students who would benefit from additional practice.

The tests I create are short and focus on what I've been modeling and students have practiced. Tests should provide you with data that informs your instructional planning. In the sections that follow, you will explore the kinds of test questions I develop—questions that apply to the diverse reading materials students use.

Guidelines for Designing Tests on Text Structure

For students to better navigate fiction and nonfiction, it's important for them to understand the elements of each and use them to think about texts. (See Forms 65–66 on the CD for a defined list of narrative and informational text elements.)

Two Ways to Evaluate Narrative Story Grammar

1. Test to evaluate students' ability to define the set of terms they have been using, such as *setting, exposition, protagonist, antagonists, plot, rising action, climax, denouement, theme, conflicts,* and *problems.* These can be short answers that define the term, or brief definitions with examples from a narrative text, such as Meg's test in Figure 5.3.

2. Test students' ability to apply specific terms to an instructional or independent reading book, to your read-aloud, or to a short text you offer them for the test. Meg's test on applying aspects of narrative story grammar to "A Hundred Bucks of Happy" by Susan Beth Pfeffer reflects her ability to apply several terms to a short story that she read specifically for this test. I prefer this type of test to simply defining terms, for definitions can be memorized, but the

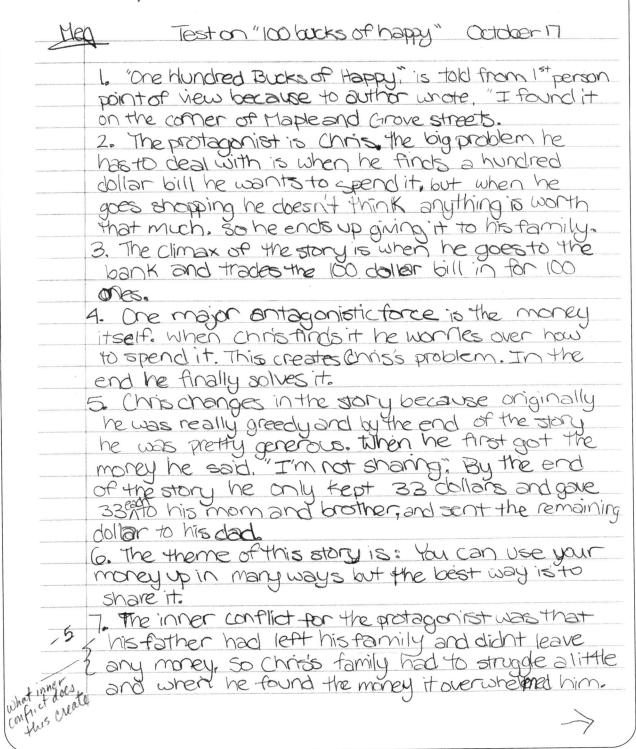

93 %

Meg   Test on "100 bucks of happy"   October 17

1. "One Hundred Bucks of Happy," is told from 1st person point of view because to author wrote. "I found it on the corner of Maple and Grove streets.

2. The protagonist is Chris, the big problem he has to deal with is when he finds a hundred dollar bill he wants to spend it, but when he goes shopping he doesn't think anything is worth that much. So he ends up giving it to his family.

3. The climax of the story is when he goes to the bank and trades the 100 dollar bill in for 100 ones.

4. One major antagonistic force is the money itself. When Chris finds it he worries over how to spend it. This creates Chris's problem. In the end he finally solves it.

5. Chris changes in the story because originally he was really greedy and by the end of the story he was pretty generous. When he first got the money he said. "I'm not sharing". By the end of the story he only kept 33 dollars and gave 33 each to his mom and brother, and sent the remaining dollar to his dad.

6. The theme of this story is: You can use your money up in many ways but the best way is to share it.

7. The inner conflict for the protagonist was that his father had left his family and didn't leave any money. So Chris's family had to struggle a little and when he found the money it overwhelmed him.

-5

what inner conflict does this create

→

Figure 5.3 Meg's test on narrative terms

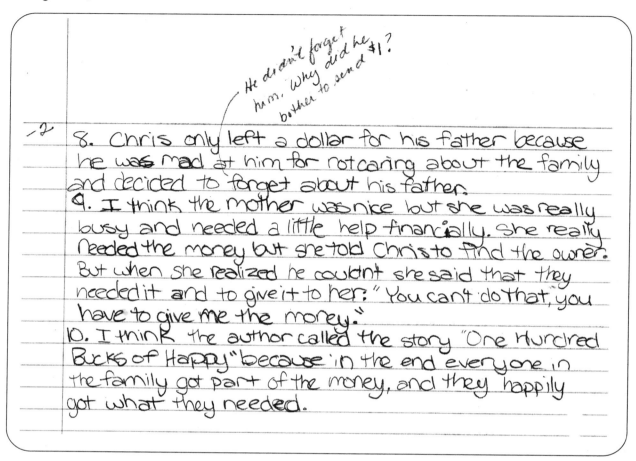

He didn't forget him. Why did he bother to send $1?

2. 8. Chris only left a dollar for his father because he was mad at him for not caring about the family and decided to forget about his father.

9. I think the mother was nice but she was really busy and needed a little help financially. She really needed the money but she told Chris to find the owner. But when she realized he couldn't she said that they needed it and to give it to her. "You can't do that, you have to give me the money."

10. I think the author called the story "One Hundred Bucks of Happy" because in the end everyone in the family got part of the money, and they happily got what they needed.

point is to see whether students can connect the definition to a part of the text. (See Forms 67–75 on the CD.)

Two Ways to Evaluate Nonfiction Text Features

1. Test to evaluate students' ability to define the set of terms they have been using: *table of contents, photographs, captions, charts, diagrams, maps, quotes, titles, headings, bold-face words and phrases, diaries, journals, news articles, posters, glossary, index, foreword,* and *afterword.* Limit the test to eight to ten features that students have learned and understand. (See Form 72 on the CD.) This means giving two separate tests so you don't overwhelm students.

2. Test to evaluate students' ability to explain why it's helpful to preview and make connections among text features before reading a chapter in a textbook or an informational picture or chapter book. (See Form 67 on the CD.)

Guidelines for Designing Reading Strategy Tests

Once you've modeled how you apply a reading strategy with your read-aloud text and students have practiced the strategy with their instructional and independent reading texts, you can invite students to show you what they know about the strategy on a test (see Form 67 on CD). Having this information helps you decide whether all students can move on to another strategy, or whether some need extra support while others can move forward.

1. Invite students to write about the strategy using these steps as guidelines:

   ◆ define the strategy;

   ◆ explain how it helps comprehension;

   ◆ list the kinds of texts it supports; and

   ◆ explain how to apply it.

2. Ask students to apply the strategy. You can have students use a section or chapter of an instructional text that they've read and discussed with a partner or you. Students note the title and author of their book and the pages used. Have students apply a strategy such as drawing conclusions about a character's personality using dialogue and the character's inner thoughts, or visualizing what they've read by drawing a picture and writing about it. In Figure 5.4, fourth-grader Lowell reads an informational text about the respiratory system while his classmate, Ethan, learns about how the tongue helps you taste (Figure 5.5). The class is studying different systems of the human body. To show understanding of this new information, Debbie Gustin, their teacher, and I ask students to visualize, in a drawing, what they've learned from specific pages in their books, then use the drawing to write. We don't tell students this is a test. Instead, we tell them we want to see how they apply the strategy they've been practicing without help from us or peers. Debbie understands that what her students can picture is what they understand; she uses this to evaluate students' understanding and note-taking.

> If you provide a short instructional-level text for assessment, students will use the entire piece to show you how they think with and apply a specific reading strategy.

Guidelines for Designing Vocabulary Tests

When students read different instructional and independent texts, it's not possible to give book-specific vocabulary tests. One way you can see how much issue-, theme-,

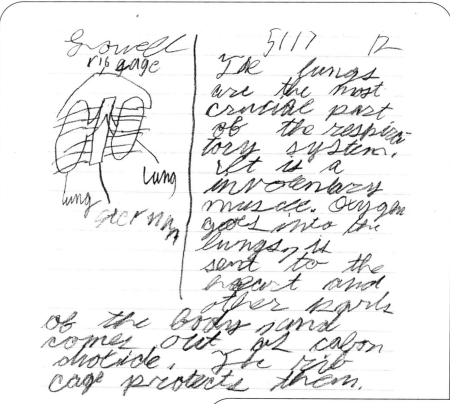

Figure 5.4 A fourth grader's test on visualizing from an informational text

Figure 5.5 A test from fourth grader Ethan, who uses his labeled drawing to write

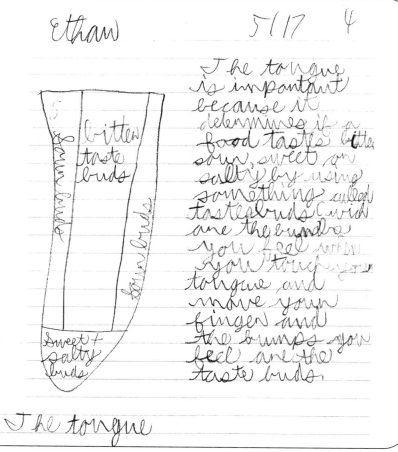

and genre-related vocabulary has been absorbed by students is to note whether they use these words in discussions, journal work, and analytical writing.

I use a concept that applies to diverse books and reading materials, such as immigration, exploration, ecology, or revolution. In addition, using their texts, students help me create a list of words related to a concept; this enlarges their vocabulary. Vocabulary tests can be nontraditional, moving beyond providing definitions to demonstrating understanding. You can ask students to complete a concept map (see Form 69 on the CD) or use words in sentences that show they comprehend meaning. At the end of a unit, I like students to complete a word map, which shows me their knowledge of the definition, features of the word, and similar words (see page 106). Word maps help groups of students review key concepts and related words and show how much they've learned.

Figure 5.6 *A fifth-grade group's word map; see Form 68 on the CD and a reproducible version on page 106*

A group of fifth graders completed this word map for *deteriorating*, a word related to their study of ecology (Figure 5.6). You can give groups a grade for their effort and the presentations of their maps, or simply offer positive feedback after each presentation.

If you study prefixes, suffixes, and Greek and Latin roots and stems, you can select words from lists that students have built and test their knowledge. It's easy to tier this type of testing by selecting different words for students to define and use in a sentence. You can also adjust the number of words you ask students to review and learn. For example, here is the list of words a seventh-grade class created for the Latin roots *jud, jur, jus*:

> *jud, judge, judgment, judicial, adjudicate, judicious, judiciously*
>
> *jur, jurisdiction, juror, jurisprudence, jury*
>
> *jus, justice, justification, injustice, just, justify*

Students studied these roots in conjunction with our theme of justice and injustice in literature. You can see how easy it would be to tier the list for both spelling and meaning.

Name _____ Date _____

Word Map

Directions:

1. Write a word or phrase that you are currently studying in the box on the left.

2. Under "What Is It?" write a similar word or phrase. Under "What Is It Like?" write some of its characteristics. Then write some examples in the space below.

3. After you complete the map, use the word in a sentence that shows you understand its meaning.

WHAT IS IT?   **WHAT IS IT LIKE?**

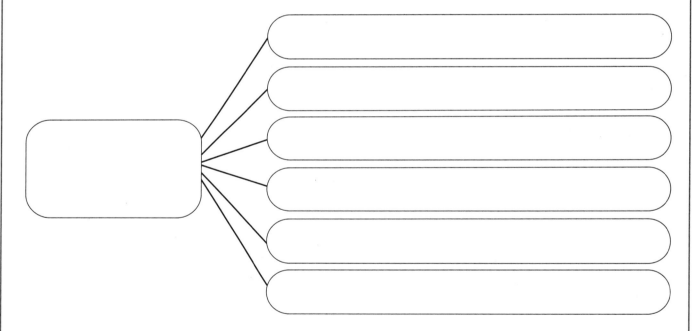

EXAMPLES:

MY SENTENCE:

Guidelines for Designing Tests Based on Journal Prompts

Since middle school teachers can have 100 to 150 students each year, it's impossible to read and grade students' journals. When I want to observe my students' thinking in their journals, I have them complete a specific journal prompt during class time. On the CD, I've included several journal prompts that students can practice and then be tested on.

Make sure you tell students they will complete a journal prompt that you'll grade. Then decide whether you want students to use their instructional or independent reading book or whether you'll use short texts. I always have students reread sections of text or all of a short text several times at home or during sustained silent reading before completing the prompt in class. Students know the prompt I'm testing in advance and can use their reading materials during the test. However, since I'm expecting preparation, I set time limits for the test because I don't want students to think they can read the selection immediately before the test. Figure 5.7 shows how eighth grader William completed the journal prompt "Problem, Actions Taken, Outcomes" using his instructional reading book, *Under a War-Torn Sky* by Laura Elliott. William does a superb job; however, he does not note the title, author, and pages the entry covered. Eighth-grader Abbie's journal entry test (see Figure 5.8) asks her to use an Isaac Asimov short story to infer two personality traits for each character and use story details to support each inference. Note her detailed and thoughtful support as well as her correct heading.

For journal prompts you can use or adapt, see pages 210–212 and 282 in my books *Differentiating Reading Instruction* and pages 371–414 in *Teaching Reading: A Differentiated Approach*.

Guidelines for Designing Essay Tests

Twice, I walked out of a final exam in college remembering that I had forgotten to include some key points in an answer. Hard experience taught me to separate the thinking from the writing when completing essay questions. It's a lesson to be passed on to middle and high school students—a lesson that affects answers and grading. Over the years, I find that adolescents resist planning all writing, including essay questions. To resolve this problem, students in my classes receive points for first jotting down notes and points for organizing the notes into a cohesive essay. Once students experience the benefits and buy into thinking first, then writing their essays, you can remove the split point system. How you divide the points between notes and the essay is your choice.

You can create essay questions that can apply to any text by using narrative elements, informational text features, issues, themes, and essential questions. I always give students the question to reflect on two to four days before the test. Doing this allows them to be thoughtful about the texts they select and gather some notes for writing in class. I usually restrict notes to both sides of one 4 x 6 index card. I require that students bring their texts and index cards to the test. It's fine if they discuss ideas with peers, as each student will use either his or her instructional or independent book for the essay.

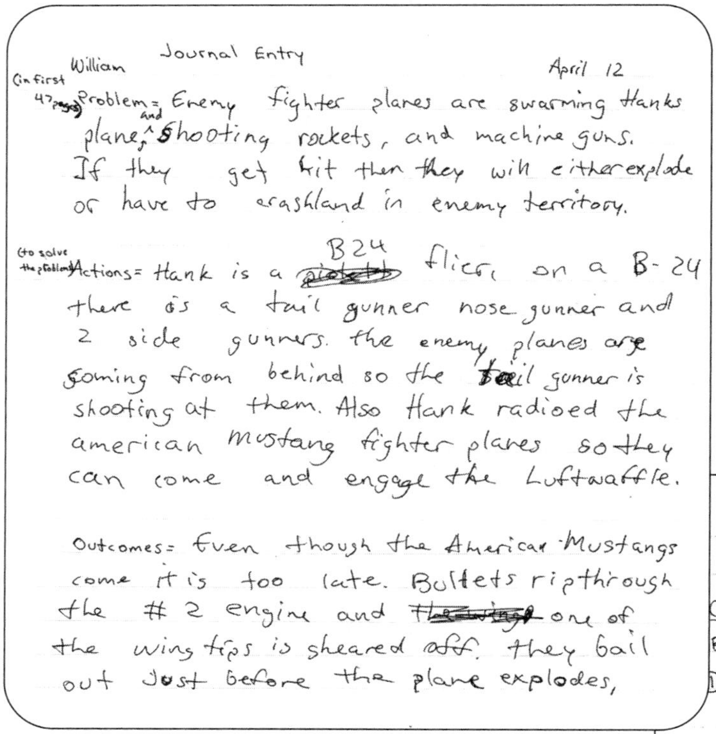

William Journal Entry April 12

(in first 47 pages) Problem = Enemy fighter planes are swarming Hanks plane, and shooting rockets, and machine guns. If they get hit then they will either explode or have to crashland in enemy territory.

(to solve the problem) Actions = Hank is a ~~pilot~~ B24 flier, on a B-24 there is a tail gunner nose gunner and 2 side gunners. the enemy planes are coming from behind so the tail gunner is shooting at them. Also Hank radioed the american Mustang fighter planes so they can come and engage the Luftwaffle.

Outcomes = Even though the American Mustangs come it is too late. Bullets rip through the # 2 engine and ~~the wing~~ one of the wing tips is sheared off. they bail out just before the plane explodes,

Figure 5.7
An eighth grader's journal text, responding to the prompt "Problem, Actions Taken, Outcome"

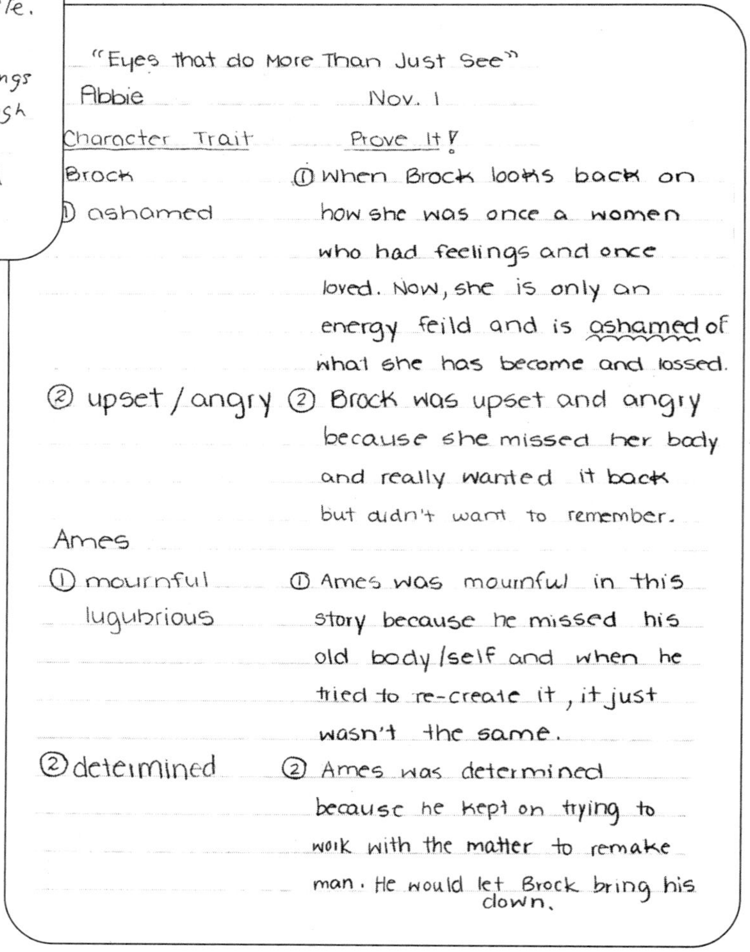

"Eyes that do More Than Just See"

Abbie Nov. 1

Character Trait	Prove It!
Brock	
① ashamed	① When Brock looks back on how she was once a women who had feelings and once loved. Now, she is only an energy feild and is ashamed of what she has become and lossed.
② upset / angry	② Brock was upset and angry because she missed her body and really wanted it back but didn't want to remember.
Ames	
① mournful lugubrious	① Ames was mournful in this story because he missed his old body/self and when he tried to re-create it, it just wasn't the same.
② determined	② Ames was determined because he kept on trying to work with the matter to remake man. He would let Brock bring his down.

Figure 5.8
An eighth grader's journal test on inferring character traits

Moreover, I'm testing thinking and creating new understandings, instead of story-specific facts. Here are five examples of open-ended essay questions:

◆ Define human rights. Choose one instructional book you read for our unit and discuss two situations that show how human rights had been violated. Were these situations righted? Explain. Include the title and author in your discussion.

◆ Growing up can be painful and joyful. Using the protagonist from two short stories that you read in this unit, show how growing up was joyful for one and painful for the other. Include the titles and authors of these short stories.

◆ Choose a recently completed independent reading book and discuss an important relationship the protagonist had with another character or person, with nature, or a situation. Explain whether the relationship was positive or negative, and whether it lasted or ended. Give reasons to support your answer. Include the title and author.

◆ Choose three antagonistic forces from one instructional text you read during this unit. Show how the forces worked against the protagonist and explain why the protagonist was able or unable to overcome each force. Include the title and author.

◆ Events, other people, and decisions can alter the course of a person's life. Choose one biography that you read for this unit. Show how an event, another person, and a decision changed that person. Include the title and author and the person's name.

Notice that I'm specific about the number of examples. This will help you grade an essay and at the same time give students much-needed guidelines for collecting details.

In Figures 5.9 through 5.12 I've included the notes and essays of two eighth graders, but removed the students' names. Here is the prompt both responded to:

In this story Francisco learns many things about life and people. Name one person and one event that taught Francisco life lessons. Use a double entry format to take notes. On the left side, note the event and person. On the right side, explain, using specific details, what Francisco learns.

Both read "Children's Game" from *The Circuit* by Francisco Jimenez. The student whose work appears in Figures 5.9 and 5.10 takes more detailed notes and uses these to craft a strong essay with a conclusion. The student whose work is featured in Figures 5.11 and 5.12 needs to collect more detailed notes in order to write a more comprehensive essay; the essay also needs a conclusion. This student will benefit from scaffolds that show how to skim a text to collect detailed notes and how to think of and include a conclusion.

Tiering Essay Tests

You can tier essay tests by placing students in different texts—texts each one can read. You can also tier tests by asking students for fewer examples or to complete two essays instead of three.

3. Event or Person	What Fran Learns
Carlos (Person)	From Carlos Francisco learns the injustice of power because he excludes Manuelito from "Kick the Can" without a reason, but because Carlos had the power Manuelito wouldn't stand up for himself.
Gabriel and the Contratista's fight (event)	From the fight between Gabriel and the Contratista Francisco learned about dignity and justice because Gabriel is willing to face the consequences to keep his dignity. like he said "He can cheat me out of my money. He can fire me. But he can't force me to what isn't right."

Notes for Essay:

Power; Childrens Game

• That Carlos needed power and that excluded Manuelito gave him power; he wasn't necessarily against him.

• People, no matter who you are, want some power; being able to influence and control others give them a sense of confidence.

Adults Game:

• contratista thought he was so much better than the migrants

Figure 5.9 *Notes for an essay test*

Long Essay:

In The Circuit chapter "Learning the Game" there were many referances to power. In the instance of the childrens game I learned that the reason that having power is so important to some people is because it gives them a sense of confidence. For mostly all people being able to influence or control someone's thoughts and actions give the person a sense of power and strength. So in the game "Kick the can" Carlos wasn't letting Manuelito play because he didn't necessarily like him, it was because knowing that he had power to influence Manuelito not to play and not stand up for himself somehow strengthened Carlo's confidence.

In this chapter it wasn't just the children dealing with power, It was also the adults. The Contratista believed he was better than and had power over Gabriel. He would "put him down" to make him feel lower (like when he told Gabriel to pull the plow, like an animal) so that he would feel higher. The contratista targeted a personal subject (his family) so that it could "hit" Gabriel hard and really upset him. Power can be for the best sometimes when its given to the right people, but in this case, it was not and therefore hurt many people as a result.

Figure 5.10 Essay written from notes in Figure 5.9

3. State Event or Person	What Fransisco learns
He learns from Carlos	He learns from Carlos that sometimes being in power, you can get mean. Like not letting Manuelito play because he was slow.
Kick the can.	Kick the can because it is just a game to have fun, play, and just be with your friends.

Figure 5.11
Notes for an essay test

Power People Hold

In the Circuit, Carlos always wanted power in almost everything he did, especially in the game kick-the-can. He was always noticed, but most kids knew him for being mean. He would yell, and wouldn't let a boy Manuelito play b/c he was slow. I think he likes being in charge. One day he finally let Manuelito play, I was happy to play and see my friend play.

In the Circuit contratista always showed greed and insensitivity. The greed was charging people a lot of money for food & rent. The insensitivity was treating Gabriel like an animal, tieing a rope around his waist and till the furrows.

Figure 5.12 *Essay written from notes in Figure 5.11*

Professional Development Suggestions

The most beneficial professional study for using tests as assessments is to share and discuss samples of students' work with colleagues at team, grade level, and/or full faculty meetings. Sharing includes the kinds of test questions, the grading system used, and samples of responses that illustrate a range of achievement. By studying one another's test designs and results, you can provide helpful feedback, gather ideas from colleagues, and explore students' performance in different subjects.

Professional books by Carol Ann Tomlinson and Rick Wormeli listed on page 89 also have suggestions for tiering, designing, and grading tests.

Scaffolding and Reteaching Chart for Tests

Task	Student Behavior	Scaffolding and Reteaching Ideas
Narrative Text Elements Tests	• Cannot define terms. • Confuses terms. • Does not know the names of narrative elements. • Unable to connect element to an example from a text.	• Reinforce with your read-alouds. • Reteach small groups, helping them learn the names of the narrative elements. • Use a graphic to help students recall the names of these elements. • Model how you connect narrative elements to a text. • Invite students in the group to take turns applying an element to their independent reading book or another text. • Use a graphic to ask students to discuss each narrative element. • Have students work with a peer or with you until they can work independently.
Nonfiction Text Features Tests	• Can name these but can't explain why each one is useful. • Has little to no knowledge of these text features. • Avoids using nonfiction text features to preview and connect, then predict or raise questions. • Does not set purposes for reading based on previewing nonfiction text features.	• Review two to three nonfiction text features with individuals or small groups. • Use a text and discuss how each feature supports reading with comprehension. • Model how nonfiction features help you preview a text, then raise questions or predict what you'll learn. • Model how previewing nonfiction text features supports setting purposes for reading. • Work to gradually release responsibility for this knowledge to students. • Pair students when using nonfiction text features so they can support one another.
Vocabulary and Concepts Tests	• Lacks the understanding of key concepts. • Has difficulty decoding or saying words. • Can't find and use context clues to figure out tough words. • Weak knowledge of roots that relate to the topic. • Weak knowledge of prefixes and suffixes. • Inadequate vocabulary for comprehending the text.	• Reteach concepts and related words to students who need this. • Reteach decoding strategies. • Model using context clues to figure out a word's meaning. • Reteach roots that relate to the topic. • Review prefixes and show how these change the meanings of words. • Scaffold until students are ready to work independently or with a peer. • Spend extra time with students whose vocabulary is weak before having them read texts with new and unfamiliar content. *(continued on next page)*

Scaffolding and Reteaching Chart for Tests, continued

Task	Student Behavior	Scaffolding and Reteaching Ideas
Reading-Strategy Tests	• Shows inability to find implied meanings. • Can define strategy but can't apply it to a text.	• Model how you apply the strategy. • Model part of the application process, then ask students to complete the process in a think aloud. • Reteach the strategy lesson using an easy text. This way students focus on the strategy. • Have students work in pairs when practicing on their own so they can help one another.
Connecting Issues, Themes, Compelling Questions Tests Journal Prompt Tests	• Understands issue and can explain it. • Has difficulty connecting these to independent or instructional reading. • Support is inadequate. • Support is general, not specific.	• Reteach the process by modeling with a read-aloud text. • Reteach using a short text that students can easily read. • Ask students to think aloud and show you their connecting process. • Continue modeling and practicing until you feel students can work with a peer. • Pair up students who continue to need practice with some support. • Reteach how to skim text for support. • Discuss the difference between general and specific support. Then, model the difference using a read-aloud text. • Provide more practice with the journal prompt during a conference with you. • Continue to support students or partners during class. Move students to independence when they show you readiness for this step.
Essay Test	• Does not take notes. • Notes need more detail. • Needs work on topic sentence/introduction. • Needs to include a conclusion.	• Have student take notes for the test question during a conference. Ask the student to think aloud so you can observe his or her process. • Offer student note-taking practice during class before writing an analytical paragraph in his or her journal. • Explain the importance of checking an essay to make sure there's a topic sentence and conclusion. • Model how the question supports framing a topic sentence. Have the student practice using other questions. • Work one-on-one in class when the student needs to gather notes with specific details. • Pair students during class work times so they can support one another. • Move students to independence when you observe they are ready.

Continue to Reflect and Wonder . . .

When you read a test, keep at the forefront of your mind what the student is doing well and what areas require extra help. Yes, tests supply us with grades. But even more important, tests enable us to identify students' strengths and areas we need to support with scaffolds or reteaching. Use the questions that follow to think about how you use tests and testing in your classes:

◆ How do my tests reflect what I'm teaching and want students to learn?

◆ What kinds of texts am I using to meet students' needs for tests?

◆ How do I have students prepare for tests?

◆ How do I ensure that students look beyond the grade to reflecting on what they did well and areas that need improvement?

◆ How do I use test results to support students who do and don't "get it"?

CHAPTER 6

Self-Evaluation: Students and Teachers Confer With Themselves

My eighth graders have thirty to forty minutes of workshop each day. During that time, they work on reading or writing. Most students use this independent work time productively; some don't. I have found that prodding students to get to work quickly becomes nagging, a teacher response that does not change the behavior of young people.

Early in my teaching journey, I learned that an effective way to change students' behaviors and choices was through self-evaluation. Workshop can start with students setting and writing goals for what they hope to accomplish. About five minutes before workshop closes, I invite students to reread their goals, discuss them, and set new goals for the next day. Or, if workshop is unproductive for too many students, I can ask them to explain what they did, then set a goal for the next day. Having something in writing gives me negotiating power. Take eighth-grader Adam's self-evaluation (see Figure 6.1). He's honest, and I find that most students are. Adam's goal shows that he will try to complete more work the next day. He's still not totally committed. The next day, with his self-evaluation in hand, I meet with Adam prior to workshop. We discuss where Adam would like to read, preferably a place with few distractions. He agrees that instead of sharing an oversized pillow with two friends, he will find a comfortable place where he can read by himself.

Eighth-grader Matt sets goals before workshop, then discusses whether he's met these (see Figure 6.2). This self-evaluation reveals Matt's strong organization and his ability to set and meet goals.

Change does not always happen quickly. For me, these short self-evaluations help students more than threats of a low grade or losing a privilege or field trip. When students must repeatedly confront their actions and decisions, and meet with you, then seventh-grader Brett's, "I prefer looking out the window to working" can transform to "I will spend most of workshop finishing my writing. I would like five minutes to look out the window or talk to Jack." When students have difficulty concentrating, when they lack stamina or the ability to focus on a task for a long time, the self-evaluations enable me to hear and honor their needs and at the same time help them inch forward in their ability to concentrate on their work.

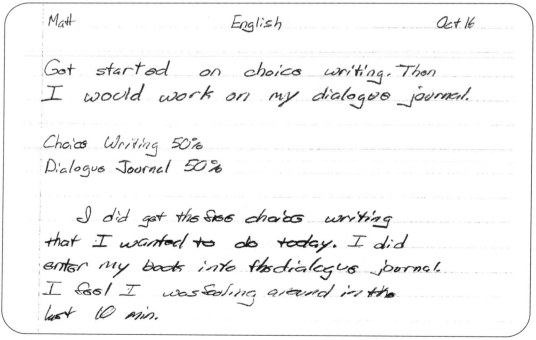

Figure 6.1 *Adam's self-evaluation and goal-setting for reading workshop*

Figure 6.2 *An eighth grader's evaluation of the goal he set for workshop time*

Keep in mind that the purpose of all self-evaluating is to raise students' awareness of their progress, their strengths, and their needs, so they can perceive their growth and recognize areas where they can improve through teacher and/or peer coaching.

As You Continue to Read . . .

In this chapter, you'll gain insights into asking students to self-evaluate to set learning goals and self-evaluate to reflect on their behavior. You'll consider how self-evaluation can develop students' independence and why it's useful when making teaching, scaffolding, and intervention decisions. Next, I'll discuss prompts and forms that support students' self-evaluation of reading, writing, collaborative projects, and independent reading as well as examples students completed. You'll reflect on peer evaluation as an outgrowth of self-evaluation that also leads to student independence.

In addition, you'll explore the benefits of teacher self-evaluations, which can

Forms for Chapter 6 That You'll Find on the CD

Student Self-Evaluation Forms

- I Used to . . . but Now I Can (Form 76)
- Preview/Set Purposes (Form 77)
- Preview/Connect/Predict (Form 78)
- Preview/Question (Form 79)
- List/Group/Label (Form 80)
- Fast Writes (Form 81)
- INSERT (Form 82)
- Predict/Support/Confirm/Adjust (Form 83)
- Questioning the Author with Nonfiction (Form 84)
- Reread and Close Read (Form 85)
- Read/Pause/Retell (Form 86)
- Visualizing (Form 87)
- Using Context Clues and Pronouncing Words (Form 88)

- Making Connections While Reading (Form 89)
- Making Inferences (Form 90)
- Determining Importance (Form 91)
- Making Connections After Reading (Form 92)
- Synthesizing (Form 93)
- Vocabulary Strategy Growth (Form 94)
- Questioning (Form 95)
- Independent Reading (Form 96)
- Progress in Reading (Form 97)
- Journal Work (Form 98)
- Content Area Strategy Checklist (Form 99)
- Journaling Checklist (Form 100)

Teacher Self-Evaluation Form

- Eleven Questions That Can Help You Self-Evaluate Your Reading Instruction (Form 101)

provide insights into your teaching and students' learning. These will include self-evaluating your planning, lessons, scaffolding, tiering, and differentiated reading instruction. Besides suggestions for professional development, the chapter will close with some thoughts about assessment, including suggestions for getting started, and "Continue to Reflect and Wonder . . ."

Student Self-Evaluation Supports Teachers and Students

Self-evaluation supports you and your students. Reading what students write about their reading, writing, and understanding can provide you with insights you might not have had otherwise. Take Ben's self-evaluation of his December–January entries on his Reading Log (see Figure 6.3). Ben's candid comments on his dislike of reading contracts and deadlines and the fact that he was reading less this year caught my attention. In a conference, Ben and I negotiated an adjustment: He would not have to abide by the minimum amount of two books a month as long as he kept reading. We also discussed how his independent reading books were quite challenging and that he might want to vary a long, tough book with an easier book on topics he loved. Indeed, Ben, one of my best English students, was a slow reader because he savored books he chose and reread parts he enjoyed. Ben's self-evaluation nudged me to work with him to remove the pressure he felt.

Students gain confidence from their self-evaluations as they note

Ben M
English   February 9

Independent Reading Logs:
  I am reading less this year.
  I do not like the reading deadlines we
  have to follow (at least 2 books) I just
  like to read at my own pace. I read
  very slowly; so having the deadlines
  makes me rush the books.
  — I like the free choice option. It allows
  me to read whatever book I choose.
  — I like the read alouds (when you or
  Mr. Ruday read to the class) It introduces
  me to different types of books that
  I generally wouldn't read.
  + My favorite types of books are: historical
  fiction, fiction, and adventure.
           The End

Figure 6.3 An eighth grader's self-evaluation of his independent reading; see Form 96 on the CD

their strengths and areas of need. Confronting areas that are challenges can start a student thinking about solving problems and helps us know whether scaffolds and reteaching are helping. Wesley, an eighth grader in my reading-writing workshop, writes about his reading progress (see Figure 6.4). Not only has Wesley become a reader, but he also recognizes that practicing reading has improved his reading rate as has choosing books he can read and enjoy. Note, too, Wesley's point that Predict/Support/Adjust and Rereading are strategies that have helped him. At a conference, I can celebrate Wesley's confidence and introduce him to other mystery and suspense writers.

> ### My Reading Progress
> Wesley
>
> Through January 22 I have read 15 books. This is more books than I have read any other year. I find that the books I am reading, I find very interesting and exiting. My favorit books to read are Adventure and scary books.
>
> When the year beggan it took me quite a while to even read a goose bumps book. But since then I have gotton much faster. Whe also have learned to Predict. support, and adjust. This stratage helps me to understand the book better, and pick out the important peices of informati
>
> I have also learnd to reread alot more so I can be shure that I understand the book, and get all the information out of it.

Figure 6.4 *An eighth grader's evaluation of his reading progress*

Use Student Self-Evaluations for Setting Goals

Goals offer students something to work toward, as long as they're reasonable and within students' reach. Students will work toward a goal they've set more readily than a goal that's imposed on them. If you have a goal in mind that a student has not recognized, meet with him or her and discuss your thoughts along with the reasons behind them. If the student buys into your suggestions, fine. If not, follow his or her suggestions, and reintroduce your thoughts later. There are times that we have to trust our students' instincts and self-knowledge, for this level of trust can bond them to us and ultimately enable us to support them.

Here is part of a conference between me and a fifth grader, Donna, that illustrates the fact that students are not always ready for our agendas. Donna, in a series of four conferences, had improved her ability to infer about characters' personalities, events, changes in characters, and decisions using realistic fiction. Donna's book log showed that she read only realistic fiction; she avoided choosing informational texts for independent reading. "Too hard. Boring," she told me. My goal during this conference was to interest Donna in informational texts and move her toward accepting a goal of choosing one on a topic she loved. I knew that our next unit would use informational books and biographies, and I wanted to introduce Donna to these.

Robb: I'm delighted that you can infer so well with realistic fiction. I'd love you to read an informational picture book on a topic you choose, then we can practice inferring with nonfiction.

Donna: I don't like those [informational books].

Robb: You might discover you'd enjoy one if it was on a topic that you cared about.

Donna: Nope. I have my next book. It's suspense.

Robb: You can read that and an informational picture book.

Donna: No thanks. Maybe later. This is choice [reading], right?

And with that last statement, Donna had checkmated me. I backed off and knew that Donna would choose realistic fiction over an informational text. I hoped that my read-alouds for this unit would show Donna the wonders of information books.

Goal-setting also gives some of the responsibility for learning to our students. Ellen, a sixth grader, sets her goals for her November reading contract. She also commits to writing dialogue entries—these will be to a classmate. Sometimes, as in Ellen's case, students provide insight into how they manage time in order to meet their goals (see Figure 6.5).

Most goal-setting in my classes occurs during one-on-one conferences. It's a

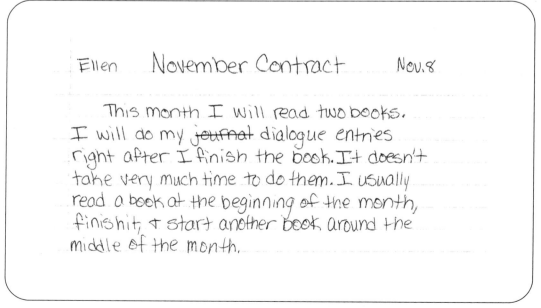

Ellen   November Contract   Nov. 8

This month I will read two books.
I will do my ~~journal~~ dialogue entries
right after I finish the book. It doesn't
take very much time to do them. I usually
read a book at the beginning of the month,
finish it, + start another book around the
middle of the month.

Figure 6.5 A sixth grader sets a monthly goal for her reading contract

natural fit with the situation, but it's not always necessary or wise to ask a student to set a goal. The language that asks students to shift direction can also be a question. Questions are kind because they show respect for the student and offer choices. Here are some sample questions that can encourage students to set goals near the end of a conference. You'll think of dozens because they'll grow out of the topic you're discussing.

- How can you improve your test scores?
- What can you do to make sure you complete and turn in homework?
- How can I help you meet instructional reading deadlines?
- What can you do to start contributing to small-group discussions?
- How can you use independent work time more effectively?
- How can you be more attentive during mini-lessons?
- What do you need to do to improve your journal writing? Book talks? Book reviews? Independent reading?

Questions can act as a catalyst for helping students set goals. However, don't expect that students will always answer your queries with the goal you wanted. And that's okay. Keep communicating with them, point out their progress and strengths, discuss and negotiate suggestions for moving forward, and listen carefully to find out where the student feels he or she can go next.

Questions can also help students decide what details they want to include in narrative self-evaluations such as Wesley's in Figure 6.4.

Questions and Prompts Help Students Self-Evaluate

If you ask students to write about their reading progress or their progress with writing about reading, you will probably receive minimal responses that won't provide specifics, such as, "I'm getting better," "I've improved," or "I'm reading more." To help students reclaim specific memories, you can select prompts and questions that link to your mini-lessons and what students have practiced.

Have students jot down notes that relate to each question or prompt they'll answer, then use their notes to compose a narrative. To help students build a mental model of what a narrative looks like, I suggest that you compose, on chart paper, a sample response that uses the questions/prompts and notes.

In the sections that follow, I've provided questions and prompts that can spark students' memories and help them take notes. Use the guidelines that follow on page 122 after you've modeled the process:

- choose questions from the boxes on pages 122, 125, 126, and 127 that indicate what you and students have focused on during the past weeks;

- write these questions on chart paper or the chalkboard;

- organize students into pairs and have partners discuss their responses to the questions;

- invite students to brainstorm or write a list of free-flowing ideas for each question they select; tell them the minimum number of questions they need to reflect on; and

- have students use their brainstorming to write about their reading process on separate paper.

Read these narratives carefully and thoughtfully so you can use the information to support students, plan lessons, and decide whether to introduce a new strategy.

Instructional Reading

Invite students to review journal work, tests, and quizzes that relate to their instructional reading. You might also want to give students a copy of a completed reading conference to review. Students can store their self-evaluations in their folders or you can store these in your literacy folders.

Questions for Students: Instructional Reading

- What strategies do I use before I read? How do these help?
- What do I do when I can't pronounce a word?
- How do I figure out the meaning of an unfamiliar word?
- How has my reading rate changed? Explain.
- Do I reread? When? Why?
- How do I help myself recall information?
- Do I set purposes? How does this help?
- How do I select the important details in a passage? chapter? book?
- What do I do if I read a section and don't recall anything?
- Do I connect my life and experiences to the book?
- When do I skim? How does this help me?
- Can I make inferences? How do I do this?
- Can I build new understandings about a topic?
- Can I write about a reading strategy so I know I understand it? Explain.

At the end of the year, Sloan reviews what he's learned in reading (see Figure 6.6). He opens by stating that his reading hasn't changed much. With the help of questions, Sloan continues his narrative, pointing out that skipping key words can affect comprehension. Sloan now has strategies for coping with unfamiliar words. He also finds reading easier and he can "know what the author is trying to say."

Writing About Reading

Having students pair-share-write during a teacher read-aloud and after group discussions can improve and enlarge their comprehension of big ideas and issues (Hernandez et al., 2006; Ivey & Fisher, 2006; Robb, 2008a). Like me, you'll want students to complete four types of journal responses that they can self-evaluate. The following are the umbrella headings for many journal entries that can be found in the binder I created, *Teaching Reading: A Differentiated Approach*.

1. Writing to build comprehension while reading. This occurs during teacher read-alouds and while students discuss and skim texts with a partner and/or a small group.

2. Writing that illustrates an understanding of the text element of fiction, such as protagonist and conflict, and nonfiction, such as sidebars and captions.

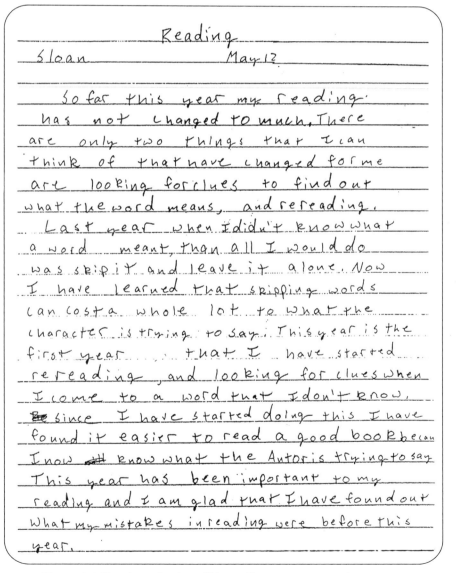

Figure 6.6 Sloan's evaluation of his reading progress over the year

3. Writing that shows students' application of reading strategies and issues to instructional and/or independent reading texts.

4. Taking notes for research or to understand key concepts, to recall important details, to have details for a summary, or to explain new words.

Mary self-evaluates her progress in journaling and points to a specific entry that shows deeper thinking (see Figure 6.7). She notes, too, that writing about reading has gotten easier. I asked Mary what she meant by "I think I finally found what I was supposed to do and I can go instantly there." She explained that after I read the story aloud, and asked the class to write about things that could cause childhood to leave, she thought about the question instead of thinking that she couldn't write a response. "When I stopped worrying about the writing and concentrated on the read-aloud, I could write about the question."

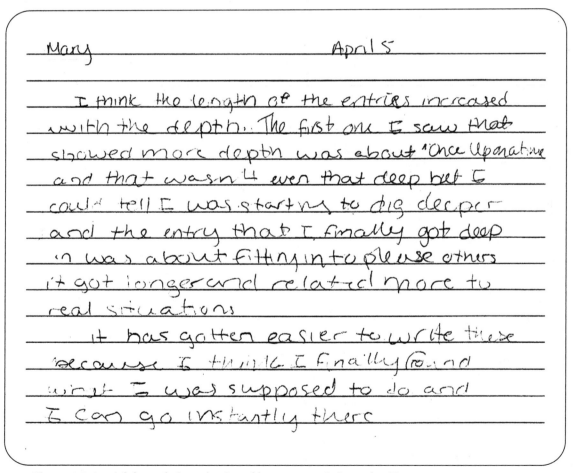

Figure 6.7 *An eighth grader's evaluation of her progress in journal writing*

Questions for Students: Writing About Reading

- How do my journal responses show that I understand what the author is telling readers?

- Do my entries for fiction and/or nonfiction show my ability to explain specific terms? Give two to three examples.

- Can I show how I connect fiction and nonfiction text features to my instructional and independent reading? Give two to three examples.

- How does a knowledge of text features improve my comprehension?

- Do my journal entries have specific examples from the text to support my ideas?

- How does writing about how I apply specific reading strategies to different texts build my reading strength?

- Why do I think my journal entries show more depth of thought over the course of the year?

- Why do or don't I feel that writing about reading improves recall and understanding?

- How do I explain key concepts, give examples, and show why the concept is important?

- How do I use notes I take for research?

- How do I use notes I take to discover important details?

- What is my most successful entry? Explain.

- What are some things that these journal entries show I've learned?

Collaborative Projects

Middle grade and middle school students are social and enjoy working on projects in small groups (Lawrence, 2007; Willis, 2007). Such projects permit students to interact while learning because they discuss decisions, ideas, materials, and deadlines. It's helpful to provide suggestions for dividing the work equitably among students. Once you've created a list that divides the project into different tasks, students can negotiate with their groups as to who will complete each task.

When students collaborate, I invite them to self-evaluate their contribution, discuss whether they met my guidelines, and grade themselves. Figure 6.8 is a self-evaluation completed by Rebecca after her participation in a collaborative venture that invited groups of eighth graders to teach a short story to the class. Note the honesty as she writes, "My journal notes are good but messy/big." She also explains that she listened carefully to her peers so she could add information that had not been presented. These evaluations help students understand what teachers consider when grading. But even more important, students see what they've learned about the goal of the project and interacting with a group.

Questions for Students: Collaborative Projects

- Can I show that I have done an equal share of the work?

- Why is listening important to collaborative projects?

- How would I evaluate my presentation?

- What was the toughest part of this project? Explain.

- What are two or three things I learned about working with others?

- Why is it important to complete my share of the project on time?

- How do my notes support this project? How does my participation in group discussions support this project?

English

Rebecca B. — Self-Evaluation — November 24

1a) My contribution for planning was good, because I made up the scenes for Charades, I made up 1 of the 3 open-ended questions for Who wants to be a good girl, and I answered 4 of the 12 short story terms so I knew them for the presentation. I also have good notes in my journal.

1b) My contribution for the presentation was okay since I wrote down some of the short story terms down on the board, and I asked a few "follow-up" questions during the short story terms.

2) My class participation during other presentations was good because I tryed to involve myself when I could if I had something that noone had already said.

3) My journal notes are good, but messy/big. In my notes I talk a little bit about what each game is going to be like, the open ended questions, and a couple short story terms. I also wrote down what the scenes would be during the Charades game.

Grade: A or (A)

Figure 6.8 *An eighth grader evaluates her contribution to a collaborative project*

Independent Reading

The amount or volume of independent, practice reading has everything to do with students' progress in reading (Block & Mangieri, 2002; Block & Reed, 2003; Krashen, 1993; Guthrie, et al, 1999; Pearson, 1993). These researchers show a positive relationship between the amount of vocabulary gain and independent reading. Like Brozo et al. (2008), they also point out that readers experience increased positive feelings toward reading and they achieve at higher levels on standardized literacy tests when they read a diversity of texts.

Questions for Students: Independent Reading

- What kinds of free choice books do I choose?

- How do I activate my prior knowledge for an independent reading book?

- Do I chat with a partner or friend to activate prior knowledge? How does this help me read my free choice books?

- Do I read at home? How often? What kinds of books?

- What does my reading log show about my interests?

- What does my reading log show about the amount of reading I do? Does this vary month to month? Explain.

- Why is independent reading important?

- Have I abandoned a book? Explain why.

- Do I have a favorite author? Genre? Explain why these have become favorites.

- Do I enjoy reading? Why or why not?

For example, Spencer, an eighth grader, reviews his reading log, tells me that he still prefers realistic fiction, appreciates being able to read books that interest him, and likes having a class library (see Figure 6.9). An important point that Spencer makes is that he appreciates teachers finding out students' interests so they can suggest books for independent reading. Spencer enjoys monthly oral book talks because he collects reading ideas from classmates.

Spencer B   April 8

During my 8th grade year at Pochatan School I have read a fair amount of books but I've only written down some of them. Here are some: The Other Side of the Truth, Athletic Shorts, Roll of Thunder Hear My Cry, Fallen Angels, Tiger Woods, El Bronx, Undone, The Farewell Kid, AAAH, Mick, and the Crowd Goes Wild, Facing the Lion, Holocaust, Go Ask Alice, and now I'm reading Under a War-Torn Sky. I really get into realistic fictions because, a lot of times they show problems that I can relate to. I also like adventurous books. Although I am a big fan and player of sports I don't particularly like sports books.

If I were a teacher, I would hand out a sheet that got into my student- finding out what kind of books he/she likes to read. Nothing is worse than reading a bad book because a 300 page good book goes faster than reading a 150 page bad book. Oral book reviews are great because they introduce all of your friends' to books which might get you to read them. I also like having a class library where you kind find a variety of books in a relatively small space.

Figure 6.9 An eighth grader evaluates his independent reading

Checklists as Self-Evaluation

With checklists you can gain insight into students' reading process by having them mull over statements that relate to what readers do before, during, and after reading. In addition to checking the strategies they use, students can explain their choices or just write about their process and feelings. I have students complete the same checklist like those on pages 130–131 three times a year: one in the first two or three weeks of school, the second in the middle of January, and the third in mid-May. With three takes of the same self-evaluative checklist, you and students can observe progress. Moreover, the first checklist provides instructional insights for you because you discover data on students' knowledge of reading strategies. This data can help you figure out students' instructional needs, assist the way you pair and/or group students, and help you decide which mini-lessons need presenting or reviewing.

I encourage students to write about their reading issues and process in all subjects. This information makes the checklist useful, for checking two to three statements gives me a small part of a student's reading portrait. Following are some comments sixth and eighth graders wrote the first time they completed checklists. Their comments give me topics for follow-up conferences; they also provide information about students' feelings toward reading, and their perceptions of what they do and don't do well.

Sixth Graders' Comments:

Fran: "I understand most of the reading given to me. The hardest part is sometimes understanding vocab words but I am getting better."

Jim: "I don't have strategies. I just read but I think it's boring."

Mike: "I read really slow. It takes lots of time. I don't enjoy it."

Eighth Graders' Comments:

Thea: "When I forget or am confused I reread but that's all."

Sara: "I sometimes read without understanding, because I'm thinking about something else."

Ryan: "I read but have no idea of what I just read."

Name _____ Date _____

A Reading Strategy Checklist

Directions:

1. Check those statements that reflect the strategies you use.

2. Write any comments you have about your reading on the back.

STRATEGIES I USE BEFORE READING:

_____ I think about the cover, title, and topic.

_____ I read the back cover and the print on the inside of the jacket.

_____ I ask questions.

_____ I predict.

_____ I skim the pictures, charts, and graphs.

_____ I read headings and boldfaced words.

_____ I think about what I know about the topic.

STRATEGIES I USE DURING READING:

_____ I stop and check to see if I understand what I'm reading.

_____ I make mental pictures.

_____ I identify confusing parts.

_____ I identify unfamiliar words.

_____ I reread to understand confusing parts and unfamiliar words.

_____ I record an unfamiliar word that I can't figure out.

_____ I use pictures, graphs, and charts to help me understand confusing parts.

_____ I stop and retell to check what I remember.

_____ I reread to remember more details.

_____ I read the captions under and above photographs, charts, and graphs.

_____ I predict and adjust as I read.

_____ I raise questions and read for answers.

STRATEGIES I USE AFTER READING:

_____ I think about why I liked or didn't like it.

_____ I retell.

_____ I speak, draw, and/or write reactions.

_____ I reread favorite parts.

_____ I reread to find details.

_____ I picture characters, places, and ideas.

_____ I predict what might happen to a character if the story continued.

Name _____ Date _____

Nonfiction Reading Strategy Checklist

Directions:

1. Check those statements that reflect the strategies you use.

2. Write any comments you have about your reading on the back.

STRATEGIES I USE BEFORE READING:

_____ I preview the section or chapter by looking and thinking about the boldfaced headings and vocabulary.

_____ I read the sentences around boldfaced words that are unfamiliar.

_____ I read the captions, charts, and graphs.

_____ I ask questions about the material.

_____ I develop a good idea about the content I will read.

_____ I review the purposes that have been set before I start reading.

STRATEGIES I USE DURING READING:

_____ I know when I'm confused and reread to understand.

_____ I continue asking questions and look for answers as I read.

_____ I look for information that relates to the purpose I've set or the teacher and class have set.

_____ I stop after each section and try to remember what I've read.

_____ I try to use clues in the sentences, charts, and pictures to figure out new words.

_____ I take notes when the reading has lots of new information.

_____ I jot down questions to ask the teacher, especially when I'm confused.

STRATEGIES I USE AFTER READING:

_____ I discuss ideas with a partner or group.

_____ I note new vocabulary in my journal.

_____ I use graphic organizers to note and organize information.

_____ I skim to find parts that might answer a question and reread these.

_____ I study my notes and skim the text after each assignment.

Why Should Teachers Self-Evaluate?

Consider two short anecdotes:

1. Out of twenty-six fifth graders in a language arts class, four do well on a reading test, ten earn C's, and the rest fail. The teacher says it's the students' fault because he's sure they didn't study enough.

2. The teacher assumes that all seventh graders understand how to determine importance when reading informational texts. When she discovers that only 10% understand this strategy, she thinks, "It's those sixth-grade teachers—they never taught this."

From these anecdotes, we can learn a lot about the need we all feel to rationalize what has occurred in our classrooms. I've come to understand that students do not absorb everything I've taught. Moreover, they might have demonstrated understanding in the past, but still need reteaching. It's important to know that we all learn from repetition. In addition, if many students fail or do poorly on a test, before assuming they did not study, it's helpful to ask students *Why?* Until our students tell us, it's impossible to assume answers. Wearing the cloak of self-evaluation can help us discover reasons, but even more important, ways to support those we teach.

Once you make self-evaluation an integral part of your teaching life, you toss aside the habit of finding people to blame when a lesson, decision, or test derails. Please understand that at times the blame voice pops into my head; I'm human. However, I've learned to shove it aside and use questions to try to deepen my understanding. Questions can come from within me (see page 132) or I can question students in a caring tone, by simply asking, *Why didn't you do your homework?* or *Why did you turn in a blank paper?*

It's all in how you view a derailed lesson or a large number of students failing a test or assignment. Your purpose should be to find out why students could not experience success on a task, or to explore ways you could improve or reteach a mini-lesson. Self-evaluation through questioning can help you better understand the situation or event and use your insights to change or adjust instruction and help students improve. Here are two questions I use after presenting a lesson: *What worked?* and *What do I feel needs improving?* These enable me to immediately gather mental feedback. While students work or during a break, I can jot down notes, especially if I feel there's lots to improve.

Name _____ Date _____

Teacher's Self-Evaluation Form: Eleven Questions That Can Help You Self-Evaluate Your Reading Instruction

1. Do I focus on what each student knows and can do well?

2. Do I discover what the student can do when working independently?

3. Do I observe the student working with a partner? With a group?

4. Do I communicate my observations to students in ways that can support their growth?

5. Do I include students when setting goals and planning interventions?

6. Do I teach and invite students to self-evaluate and use these to support their learning?

7. Do I accept students' feelings and attitudes toward reading and learning? Can I get beyond negatives and try to transform some of these into positives?

8. Do I offer enough practice of a strategy for students to experience its benefits and apply it to their own reading?

9. Do I provide opportunities for students to transfer their knowledge of how a strategy works to a variety of reading materials?

10. Do I use peers to support each other?

11. Do I record some of my observations using sticky notes or checklists and use them to evaluate progress, plan instruction, and inform parents and administrators?

What Can Teachers Self-Evaluate?

Here is a list of what you can self-evaluate. Avoid limiting yourself to this list, for you will find many other situations that need reflection. Developing the self-evaluative stance can help you meet students' needs and help you improve your planning and instruction.

Self-evaluation is an ongoing process and can include:

- a lesson that you presented
- your daily lesson plans
- your unit plans that cover four to eight weeks of instruction
- a conference between you and a student
- the quality of test questions
- results of a test or quiz
- the quality of homework
- your classroom library
- journaling requirements and responses
- students' listening skills
- students' use of independent work time
- matching instructional texts to students
- your grading policy
- a meeting with your principal or supervisor
- a parent conference
- a program you're involved in, such as peer mentoring
- your knowledge base of a topic such as reading strategies
- a staff development workshop
- a relationship with a colleague

Professional Development Suggestions

In my opinion, the best way to learn more about student and teacher self-evaluations is to share them with colleagues during team, grade level, or full faculty meetings. Ask two to four teachers to volunteer to bring self-evaluations to a meeting for the group to study and discuss. This allows you to see what others are doing and develop a process for reading the evaluations and offering feedback. When I'm facilitating these meetings, I have the group point out and discuss:

- statements that show progress;
- statements and phrases that illustrate confidence;
- statements the indicate a need for additional support;
- possible scaffolds;
- the tone of the piece (whether it is positive or negative and why); and
- the points you might discuss with this student in a follow-up conference.

You and colleagues can read and discuss articles on assessment from professional journals and books. These will supply you with new ideas and validate your practices. The box on page 134 suggests journals and books to investigate.

Continue to Reflect and Wonder . . .

It's tough to find the time to weave self-evaluation into your school day. But it's important. And you don't have to make self-evaluation a daily happening. Start by choosing one area—instructional or independent reading, collaborative projects, or journaling about reading—and focus on it. Start by asking students to complete two to four self-evaluations during a school year. Once you're comfortable, you can juggle two areas. The questions that follow can help you reflect on the power of you and students using self-evaluations to grow and improve:

◆ Why do I feel self-evaluation is an important part of assessment?

◆ How do I model using questions to self-evaluate?

◆ How do students benefit from self-evaluation?

◆ How can self-evaluation support my teaching and learning?

Professional Materials on Assessment

Three journals to explore:

- *Educational Leadership* published by ASCD, the Association for Supervision and Curriculum Development, 1703 North Beauregard Street, Alexandria, Virginia 22311-1714.

- *Language Arts* published by the National Association of Teachers of English, 111 W. Kenyon Road, Urbana, IL 61801-1096.

- *The Reading Teacher* published by the International Reading Association. 800 Barksdale Road, P.O. Box 81398, Newark, DE 19714-8139.

Professional books to explore:

- *Assessing Readers: Qualitative Diagnosis and Instruction* by Rona A. Flippo, Heinemann, 2003.

- *Conferring with Readers: Supporting Each Student's Growth and Independence* by Jennifer Serravallo and Gravity Goldberg, Heinemann, 2007.

- *More Ways to Handle the Paper Load: On Paper and Online*, Jeffrey N. Golub, editor, National Council of Teachers of English, 2005.

- *Scientific Reading Assessment* by Maryann Manning, Heinemann , 2006.

- *Strategies for Reading Assessment and Instruction: Helping Every Child Succeed*, Third Edition by D. Ray Reutzel and Robert B. Cooter, Jr., Pearson, Merrill/Prentice Hall, 2007.

A Quick Reference Guide to Reading Strategies

The following chart contains a list of the strategies for which I have included an assessment form. I define each strategy briefly here; for more detailed descriptions and strategy lessons, see my books *Teaching Reading: A Differentiated Approach* (2008) or *Teaching Reading in Middle School* (2000).

Before Reading

Strategy	Thumbnail Explanation
Select Books for Independent Reading	Choosing readable books that can support growth in fluency, word knowledge, and comprehension, and enlarge background knowledge. Use the two-finger strategy: select a book that has only two words on a page that students can't pronounce or whose meaning is unknown.
Use Knowledge of Genres	Accessing what they already know about text structures to support the meaning-making process.
Preview/Set Purposes	Using their preview of nonfiction or fiction, students set purposes for reading. With nonfiction, preview text features. With fiction, preview title, cover illustration, and first one to two pages of a chapter.
Preview/Connect/Predict	Using nonfiction text features, students make connections among features and to what they know about a topic. Then, students use this preview to set three to four purposes for reading.
Preview/Question	Using their preview of fiction or nonfiction, students raise questions about the content, text structure, what they think they'll learn. These questions drive the reading.

List/Group/Label	Accessing and brainstorming what they already know about a topic, concept, or issue, students work in pairs or small groups to organize their ideas into related groups, then create a heading that categorizes each group of ideas. Works well when students have some prior knowledge.
Fast Writes	Writing what they recall about a topic, genre, issue, or concept allows students and teachers to discover what students know. Fast writes have a time limit, usually two to three minutes. Students write without stopping; if they get stuck, they repeat the last word they wrote until an idea pops into their minds. Works well when students have some prior knowledge.

During Reading

Strategy	Thumbnail Explanation
Predict/Support	Making predictions while reading, then finding evidence that supports predictions.
Confirm/Adjust	Using data gathered while reading to confirm or adjust predictions.
Visualize	Increasing comprehension and recall by creating mental pictures of information, vocabulary, and elements of fiction.
Read/Pause/Retell/ Read On or Reread	Recognizing what is and is not understood while reading by retelling chunks of text, then checking to makes sure students recall many details. Students can read on or reread to improve understanding and recall.
INSERT: Interactive Notations System for Effective Reading and Thinking	Self-monitoring using specific notations to help students continually check what they do and do not understand and recall while reading. Students can access a fix-up strategy such as close read to improve comprehension of confusing passages.
Questioning the Author (QtA)	Using queries designed by Beck & McKeown (2006), teachers ask students questions from the list created by the authors with the goal of starting a discussion that explores the author's message, purpose, and/or big ideas. Used with materials students have not read.
Close Read	Having students return to a confusing phrase, sentence, or passage and reread it slowly and carefully to build comprehension. Students can bring what they know or are learning to connect ideas between sentences, figure out confusing pronoun references, and try to discover the author's meaning and purposes.

Vocabulary and Context Clues	Using clues in the text or in nonfiction features to figure out the meaning of an unfamiliar word.
Make Personal Connections	Relating their experiences and prior knowledge to information in the text enables students to connect on a personal level.

After Reading

Strategy	Thumbnail Explanation
Make Connections Beyond Self	Linking themes on a completed book to other books, the Internet, videos and films, and to issues and problems in their family, school, neighborhood, and the world.
Make Inferences	Using what you know about a topic or genre to discover unstated or implied meanings in texts.
Determining Importance	Setting purposes before reading to support finding important details in a text after reading.
Synthesize	Summarizing information from large sections of text. Forming new positions and opinions as learners read more and more text.
Visualize	Increasing comprehension and recall by creating mental pictures of information, vocabulary, and elements of fiction after reading.
Vocabulary Growth	Completing various graphic organizers that demonstrate students knowledge of new concepts and related vocabulary.

Some Excellent Magazines and Newspapers

Students enjoy magazines because articles are usually short and contain many interesting photographs, illustrations, maps, puzzles, diagrams, and charts. Here are some excellent resources:

Calliope is a 48-page, themed magazine about people and events of the past. *Cobblestone Publishing, 7 School St., Peterborough, NH 03458*

Cobblestone is a 48-page, theme-related magazine. It offers an imaginative approach to teaching history and those people, events, and ideas that have shaped the American experience. *Cobblestone Publishing, 7 School St., Peterborough, NH 03458*

Field & Stream, Jr. has articles on conservation, hunting, fishing, sporting ethics, and nature. *Times Mirror Magazines, 2 Park Ave., New York, NY*

Ranger Rick helps deepen children's understanding of nature. *National Wildlife Federation, 8925 Leesburg Pike, Vienna, VA 22184-001*

Scholastic Dynamath contains 16 pages of word problems, test prep ideas, and computation for grades 5 and 6. *Scholastic, 557 Broadway, New York, NY 10012*

Scholastic Math has articles that offer strategies for problem solving, computation, statistics, test prep, consumer math, and real-life math applications for grades 7 to 9. *Scholastic, 557 Broadway, New York, NY 10012*

Scholastic News is a weekly classroom newspaper for students in grades 3 to 6. *Scholastic, 557 Broadway, New York, NY 10012*

Scholastic Scope is a language arts magazine that presents plays, interviews, poetry, fiction, and nonfiction for students in grades 6 to 10. *Scholastic, 557 Broadway, New York, NY 10012*

Science Weekly motivates students to learn about their world and develops science and technology awareness. Available for grades 3 to 8. *Science Weekly, 2141 Industrial Parkway, Suite 202, Silver Spring, MD 20904*

Science World is published biweekly and has several feature articles and brief newsworthy items based on current research in all the sciences. It is ideal for grades 7 to 10. *Scholastic, 557 Broadway, New York, NY 10012*

The Wall Street Journal, Classroom Edition is for students in grades 7 to 12 and tries to improve their business and economic literacy. *The Wall Street Journal, Classroom Edition, P.O. Box JJ, Sonoma, CA 95476*

Zoobooks offer entertaining and informative full-color articles about wildlife and is ideal for students in grades 3 to 8. *Wildlife Education Limited, 3590 Kettner Blvd., San Diego, CA 92101*

Complete List of Forms on the CD

Chapter 4: Assessing Tiered Learning Tasks *Forms 43–61*

Chapter 5: Assess by Testing What You Teach *Forms 62–75*

Chapter 6: Self Evaluation *Forms 76–101*

* *These forms are customizable; you may enter student data on the form and save it to a file.*

To view and print the files on the CD, you will need to download Adobe Reader™, version 7.0 or higher. This download is available free of charge for Mac and PC systems at www.adobe.com/products/acrobat/readstep2.

Bibliography of Professional Literature

Afflerbach, P. (2007). *Understanding and using reading assessment, K-12.* Newark, DE; International Reading Association.

Allington, R. (2006a). Fluency: Still waiting after all these years. In S.J., Samuels & A.E. Farstrup (Eds.), *What research has to say about fluency instruction.* Newark: DE: International Reading Association.

Allington, R. (2006b). Intervention all day long: New hope for struggling readers. *Voices From the Middle, 14*(4), 7-14.

Allington, R. (2002). What I've learned about effective reading instruction. *Phi Delta Kappan, 83*(10), 740-747.

Allington, R. (2001). *What really matters for struggling readers: Designing research-based programs.* Boston: Allyn & Bacon.

Allington, R., & Cunningham, P. M. (2002). *Schools that work: Where all children read and write.* (2nd ed.) Boston: Allyn & Bacon.

Ambruster, B.B., Lehr, F., & Osborn, J.M. (Eds.) (2001). *Put reading first: The research building blocks for teaching children to read.* Washington, D.C.: The National Institute for Literacy.

Anderson, R. (1984). Role of readers' schema in comprehension, learning, and memory. In R. Anderson, J. Obscures, & R. Tierney (Eds.), *Learning to read in American schools.* Hillsdale, NJ: Lawrence Erlbaum Associates.

Anderson, R., Wilson, P., & Fielding, L. (1988). Growth in reading and how children spend their time outside of school. *Reading Research Quarterly, 23*: 285-303.

Anderson, V. (1992). A teacher development project in transactional strategy instruction for teachers of severely reading-disabled adolescents. *Teaching & Teacher Education*, pp. 391–403.

Armstrong, S. (2008). *Teaching smarter with the brain in focus.* New York: Scholastic.

Bambrick-Santoyo, P. (2008). Data in the driver's seat. *Educational Leadership, 65*(4), 43-46.

Beck, I.L., & McKeown, M.G. (2006). *Improving comprehension with questioning the author.* New York: Scholastic.

Block, C. C., & Mangieri, J. N. (2002). Recreational reading: Twenty years later. *The Reading Teacher, 55*(6), 572-586.

Block, C. C., & Reed, K. M. (2003). *Trade books: How they significantly increase students' vocabulary comprehension, fluency, and positive attitudes toward reading* (Research Report No. 1734-004). Charlotte, NC: Institute for Literacy Enhancement.

Brozo, W.G., Shiel, G., Topping, K. (2008) Engagement in reading: Lessons learned from three PISA countries. *Journal of Adolescent & Adult Literacy, 51*(4), 304-317.

Buehl, D. (2001). *Classroom strategies for interactive learning.* Newark, DE: International Reading Association.

Caldwell, J.S. (2008). *Reading assessment.* (2nd ed.) New York: Guildford.

Clay, M. (1993). Marie Clay responds . . . *Reading in Virginia,* 18, 1–3.

Dowhower, S.L. (1999). Supporting a strategic stance in the classroom: A comprehension framework for helping teachers help students to be strategic. *The Reading Teacher,* (57), 672-688.

Duke, N. K., & Pearson, P. D. (2002). Effective practices for developing reading comprehension. In A.E. Farstrup & S. J. Samuels (Eds.), *What research has to say about reading instruction.* Newark, DE: International Reading Association.

Fisher, D., & Frey, N. (2007). *Checking for understanding: Formative assessment techniques for your classroom.* Arlington, VA: ASCD.

Gambrell, L.B. (2007). Reading: Does practice make perfect? *Reading Today. 24*(6), 16.

Gardner, H. (1999). *Intelligence reframed: Multiple intelligences for the 21st century.* New York: Basic Books.

Gardner, H. (1991). *The unschooled mind: How children think and how schools should teach.* New York: Basic Books.

Gillet, J. W., & Temple, C. (2000). *Understanding reading problems: Assessment and instruction.* New York: Longman.

Goodman, Y. (1985). Kidwatching: Observing children in the classroom. In A. Jaguar & M. T. Smith-Burke (Eds.). *Observing the language learner.* Newark, DE: International Reading Association.

Guthrie, J. T., & Wigfield, A. (2000). Engagement and motivation in reading. In M.L. Kamil, P. B. Mosenthal, P.D. Pearson, & R. Barr (Eds.) *Handbook of reading research.* Mahwah, NJ: Erlbaum.

Guthrie, J. T., Wigfield, A., Metsala, J., & Cox, K. (1999). Motivational and cognitive predictions of text comprehension and reading amount. *Scientific Studies of Reading, 3*(3), 231-256.

Guthrie, J. T. (2004). Teaching for literacy engagement (Vol. III, pp. 403-422). *Journal of Literacy Research, 36*, 1-30.

Harvey, S. & Goudvis, A. (2000). *Strategies that work.* Portsmouth, NH: Heinemann.

Hernandez, A., Kaplan, M. A., & Schwartz, R. (2006). For the sake of argument. *Educational Leadership, 64*(2), 48-52.

Ivey, G., & Fisher, D. (2006). When thinking skills trump reading skills. *Educational Leadership, 64*(2), 16-21.

Keene, E. & Zimmerman, S. (2007). *Mosaic of thought.* (2nd ed). Portsmouth, NH: Heinemann.

Krashen, S. (1993). *The power of reading: Insights from the research.* Englewood, CO: Libraries Unlimited.

Langer, G.M., Cotton, A.B., & Goff, L.S. (2003). *Collaborative analysis of student work: Improving teaching and learning.* Alexandria, VA: ASCD.

Lawrence, M. (2007). Students as scientists: Synthesizing standards-based with student-appropriate instruction. *Educational Leadership, 38*(4), 30-37.

Marzano, R. J. (2004). *Building background knowledge for academic achievement: Research on what works in schools.* Alexandria, VA: ASCD.

McTighe, J., & O'Conner, K. (2006). Seven practices for effective learning. *Educational Leadership, 63*(93), 10-17.

Nagy, W. & Anderson, R. (1984). How many words are there in printed school English? *Reading Research Quarterly, 19*: 304-330.

Nokes, J. (2008). The observations/inference chart: Improving students' abilities to make inferences while reading nontraditional texts. *Journal of Adolescent & Adult Literacy, 51*(7), 538-546.

Pearson, P.D. (1993). Teaching and learning reading: A research perspective. *Language Arts, 70*, 502-511.

Popham, W.J. (2003). *Test better, teach better: The instructional role of assessment.* Arlington, VA: ASCD.

Power, B. (1996). *Taking note: Improving your observational note taking.* York, ME: Stenhouse.

Reutzel, D.R., & Gikkubsworht, P.M. (1991). Reading time in school: Effect on fourth graders' performance on a criterion-referenced comprehension test. *Journal of Educational Research, 84*, 170-176.

Robb, L. (2008a). *Differentiating reading instruction: How to teach reading to meet the needs of each student.* New York: Scholastic.

Robb, L. (2008b). *Teaching reading: A differentiated approach.* New York: Scholastic.

Robb, L. (2004). *Nonfiction writing from the inside out.* New York: Scholastic.

Robb, L. (2003). *Teaching reading in social studies, science, and math.* New York: Scholastic.

Robb, L. (2000). *Teaching reading in middle school: A strategic approach to teaching reading that improves comprehension and thinking.* New York: Scholastic.

Snow, C.E., Burns, M.S., & Griffin, P. (1998). *Preventing reading difficulties in young children.* Washington, D.C.: National Academy Press.

Sousa, D.A. (2001). *How the brain works.* Thousand Oaks, CA: Corwin Press.

Sternberg, R. J. (2008). Assessing what matters. *Educational Leadership, 65*(4), 20-26.

Tierney, R., & Readence, J. (2000). *Reading strategies and practices: A compendium.* Boston, MA: Allyn & Bacon.

Tomlinson, C. (2004). *How to differentiate instruction in mixed-ability classrooms.* (2nd ed.) Arlington, VA: ASCD.

Tomlinson, C. A. (1999). *The differentiated classroom: Responding to the needs of all learners.* Alexandria, VA; ASCD.

Tomlinson, C.A., & Cunningham, E.C. (2003). *Differentiation in practice: A resource guide for differentiation curriculum—grades 5–9.* Alexandria, VA: ASCD.

Vaughan, J., & Estes, T. (1986). *Reading and reasoning beyond the primary grades.* Boston, MA: Allyn & Bacon.

Vygotsky, L. (1978). *Mind in society: The development of higher psychological processes.* Cambridge, MA: Harvard University Press.

Willis, J. (2007). Cooperative learning is a brain turn-on. *Educational Leadership, 38*(4), 4-13.

Woods, M. & Moe, A. (1999). *Analytical reading inventory.* (6th ed.) Saddle River, NJ: Merrill.

Wormeli, R. (2007). *Differentiation: From planning to practice Grades 6-12.* York, ME: Stenhouse.

Wormeli, R. (2006). *Fair isn't always equal: Assessing & grading in the differentiated classroom.* York, ME: Stenhouse.

Bibliography of Children's Literature

Avi. (1993). *Nothing but the truth: A documentary novel.* New York: Avon Flare Books.

Byars, B. (2000). *The midnight fox.* New York: Scholastic.

Christopher, M. (2005). *Legends in sports: Babe Ruth.* New York: Little Brown.

Curtis, C.P. (1995). *The Watsons go to Birmingham–1963.* New York: Scholastic.

Davidson, M. (1971). *Louis Braille: The boy who invented books for the blind.* New York: Scholastic.

Fletcher, R. (2005). *Marshfield dreams.* New York: Henry Holt.

Hamilton, V. (2006). *M.C. Higgins the great.* New York: Alladin.

Kraske, R. (1973). *Harry Houdini: Master of magic.* New York: Scholastic.

Le Guin, U. (1988). *Catwings.* Illustrated by S.D. Schindler. New York: Scholastic.

Lowry, L. (1993). *The giver.* Boston, MA: Houghton.

McGovern, A. (1978). *Shark lady: True adventures of Eugenie Clark.* New York: Scholastic.

McKissack, P.C., & McKissack, F. (1993). *Sojourner Truth: Aint' I a woman?* New York: Scholastic.

Naylor, P.R. (2000). *Shiloh.* New York: Aladdin.

Paterson, K. (1987). *The great Gilly Hopkins.* New York: HarperTrophy.

Pfeffer, S. B. (1987). A hundred bucks of happy. In Donald R. Gallo (Ed.), *Visions.* New York: Dell.

Ryan, P.M. (2000). *Esperanza rising.* New York: Scholastic.

Soto, G. (1990). Seventh grade. In *Baseball in April,* Orlando, FL: Harcourt Brace.

Spinelli, J. (1997). *The library card.* New York: Scholastic.

Wolf, V.E. (2006). *Make lemonade.* New York: Henry Holt.